COOK:30

www.cook30.com

Copyright © Revive Concepts Limited 2015
Published & Distributed by Revive Concepts Limited
Partnering with Three Angels Broadcasting Network
First printing 2015 (this book).

ISBN: 978-1-934869-99-4

Also by Jeremy Dixon: **The Revive Cafe Cookbook**
The Revive Cafe Cookbook 2
The Revive Cafe Cookbook 3
The Revive Cafe Cookbook 4

Produced in New Zealand & USA. Printed in China.
Food Preparation, Styling & Photography: Jeremy Dixon
Programme Photography: Verity Dixon
Graphic Design: Rebecca Zwitser, Jeremy Dixon
Book Assembly: Verity Dixon, Nyree Tomkins
Proof Readers: Nyree Tomkins, Verity Dixon, Dawn Simpson, Heather Cameron, Kjirstnne Jensen
Show concept created and produced by: Shelley Quinn, Jeremy Dixon, Rodney Laney
Set design and construction: Jeremy Dixon, Shelley Quinn, Scott Ellis, RobbieD Lauterjung, Dave Turner, Brandon Tygret.
Cook:30 Logo: Kyle Warren
Lighting: Ademar Neto, Jeremy Dixon

The publisher makes no guarantee as to the availability of the products in this book. Every effort has been made to ensure the accuracy of the information presented and any claims made; however, it is the responsibility of the reader to ensure the suitability of the product and recipe for their particular needs. Many natural ingredients vary in size and texture, and differences in raw ingredients may marginally affect the outcome of some dishes. All health advice given in this book is a guideline only. Professional medical or nutritional advice should be sought for any specific issues.

Imperial and metric measurements have been used in this cookbook. The tablespoon size used is ½fl oz (15ml), teaspoon $\frac{1}{6}$fl oz (5ml) and cup 8fl oz (250ml). Some countries use slightly different sized measurements, however these should not make a significant difference to the outcome of the recipes.

Revive Cafe/Revive Concepts Contact:
P O Box 12-887, Penrose, Auckland 1642, New Zealand
Email: jeremy@revive.co.nz Phone: +64 (9) 303 0420
www.revive.co.nz

3ABN Contact:
P O Box 220, West Frankfort, IL 62896, USA
Phone: +1 (618) 627 4651
www.3abn.org

If you like the recipes in this book I recommend you sign up for my weekly inspirational Revive e-mails.
They contain a weekly recipe, cooking and lifestyle tips, the weekly Revive menu, special offers and Revive news.
Visit www.revive.co.nz to sign up.
Privacy Policy: Revive will never share your details and you can unsubscribe at any time.
LIKE us on Facebook to get more recipes and health tips! www.facebook.com/cafe.revive

COOK:30

**CREATE DELICIOUS WHOLEFOOD PLANT-BASED
MEALS FROM SCRATCH IN JUST 30 MINUTES**

Introduction

Cook:30 Philosophy

This cookbook is all about how I cook at home.

It uses the recipes from my Revive Cafes and Revive Cafe Cookbooks, and combines them to create a complete meal in just 30 minutes.

After running two successful vegetarian cafes for 10 years I have learned how to prepare food quickly and inject a lot of flavour without adding costly or unhealthful ingredients.

I am not a nutritionist and do not get into the finer points of dietary philosophy (of which there is plenty debate). But believe in using simple, wholegrain plant based food in my own diet, at home, in my cookbooks and cafes.

This means lots of fresh fruit and vegetables. Whole grains like brown rice, oats, quinoa. Plant-based proteins like beans, nuts, lentils and tofu. And making it taste awesome with international flavours and plenty of herbs and spices. Simple.

I do not use meat, dairy, seafood. I do not use white sugar, white flour or other highly processed ingredients. I avoid preservatives where I can. And while they do have their place on occasions, I do not use processed meat substitutes.

My natural recipe selection, preparation shortcuts and rustic presentation style would be scorned in most high level fine dining restaurants and cooking schools. However in a home (and casual cafe setting) they are quick to make, healthful and look and taste awesome!

How Cook:30 was born

After meeting me and viewing my cookbooks in New Zealand, Brenda Walsh invited me as a guest cook on her 3ABN Today programme with her sisters in 2013. My wife Verity and I travelled to the US to film this and we had a lot of fun sharing some Revive meals on their programme.

About that time Shelley Quinn (Program Development Manager) was looking for a new cooking programme for the 3ABN channel. Shelley asked me to share with her my vision for a cooking programme.

I explained that I would love to do a programme that would portray the way I cook at home.

Rather than having pre-measured ingredients sitting nicely on the counter ready for use, there would be multi-tasking, taking ingredients from the fridge and shelves, throwing in "approximate" amounts, and having several pots on the stove at once.

Everything would be made from scratch and I would not use canned vegetarian meals or specialist products – just common healthy plant-based foods that are readily available everywhere in the world.

It would have a lot of close-up shots and be fast-paced just like a cafe or home kitchen.

While this type of programme would surely be more work, it would more accurately reflect my style of cooking and would help viewers get a realistic picture of how they can cook healthy wholefood plant-based meals at home.

I thought perhaps my vision for the programme may be too much of a departure from other 3ABN cooking shows, however Shelley loved the concept and we immediately agreed to produce the series together.

To make it even easier for people to adopt these new cooking skills, I decided it would be great to do a cookbook which is what you are now holding.

All of the photographs in this book were shot during the taping of the Cook:30 programmes.

My mission

It is my mission in life to share with people how to eat and cook healthy. If you choose to put healthy food in your mouth, you will have a healthier body, get sick less often, reduce your chances of getting lifestyle diseases, and most likely live a lot longer.

However over and above those reasons, the best part about eating and living healthy is that you will have so much energy and vitality, feel great, and be able to achieve your dreams in life!

So give it a go, it is worth making the change, and I hope in this book and TV series that you will see how simple it can be.

I would love to hear how you find these recipes and how they impact your life.

Jeremy Dixon
jeremy@revive.co.nz

Contents

Episode Overview

Revive Cafes

In 2003 my wife, Verity, and I treated ourselves to a 10 day cleanse at a health retreat. We had steam baths, massages, days of juice fasting, long walks, nutritional education, cooking classes, naturopathic consultations and 10 days of rest. We came back with a newfound vitality and zest for life.

By implementing simple changes in the ensuing months such as healthy eating, drinking plenty of water and exercise, we just felt so good!

However we realised on returning to Auckland that most cafes and eating places served food that was not really good for you.

I had a great career working for Sanitarium Health Food Company in Auckland for 10 years, as a marketer of healthy breakfast cereals like Weet-Bix. I had always had the dream of becoming a chef or owning a cafe, so in late 2004 I took a bold and risky move and decided to leave my great job to open a healthy cafe.

I quickly faced some hard realisations in researching successful food outlets. In order to be successful in hospitality it appeared that you needed to serve coffee, alcohol, soft drinks, sugary cakes, food full of white flour and be open long hours in the weekends. Against the advice of several people, I decided that I could not sleep at night serving people these kinds of food and beverages, and I continued on in search of a suitable location.

I purchased an existing cafe on Fort St and spent 2 months renovating, painting, organising and setting up my new cafe.

Thinking I knew it all from my Sanitarium career, I had to quickly learn the smarts of hospitality. It took a very stressful 12 months of menu amending, roster changing, marketing and staff training. However, I stuck at it, and eventually managed to get our formula working right.

We had queues out the door most lunchtimes and it made me very happy to know that so many people desired to eat heathy. It was a very intense 12 months, but the biggest thing I learned from this was to keep trying new things and to stick at it.

The cafe was so successful we opened a second Revive Cafe on Lorne St in 2008, just one kilometer uptown from my first cafe. Also in 2013 my lease ran out in my Fort St cafe and I moved a block away to Wyndham St to a location twice the size, where we now also have our central kitchen.

Revive has a salad bar with the options changing weekly. We serve a meal of the day, a hotpot of the day and a dahl of the day. We also serve a frittata of the week and soup of the week and some delicious healthy sweets and smoothies.

I have a passion for sharing health principles with people. So many people are dragging themselves through life content with being overweight, having headaches, health issues and feeling tired all the time.

I put a lot of time into our Revive weekly e-mails which include health tips and recipes. I also do cooking demonstrations where I share how simple it is to make healthy food, and have produced a series of cookbooks which are another way to share the recipes we use at Revive and to help people learn how to prepare healthy meals themselves.

I hope to see you at Revive sometime!

The 8 Keys to Healthy Living

These are the health principles that Revive Cafe and my life are founded on.

It is not enough to just eat healthy food in order to have complete energy and vitality. There are other simple things that create good health, and they are summarised by these 8 keys. They are easy to remember, they spell "NEWSTART".

The good news is that if you apply these simple 8 steps in your day-to-day living, you will notice dramatic improvements in your vitality, health and quality of life.

If you do not have great health and do not wake up each morning full of energy, chances are that you are not following some of these principles. Go through this list and start to implement one extra principle a week.

However, don't stop there, sign up for the regular Revive emails at www.revive.co.nz for weekly inspirational ideas and encouragement.

Disclaimer

Please note that these are general lifestyle principles only and it is recommended that you see a health professional regarding any serious health issues.

Fuel your body with quality food and feel great!

Good nutrition is all about putting fresh, quality, alive foods into your body. Make sure a large proportion (ideally 50-70%) of your diet is fresh, raw fruit and vegetables.

All good things in moderation and set yourself free from harmful things!

We all know that drugs, cigarettes, caffeine and alcohol are bad for our health and will shorten out lives. Our bodies are much better off if we avoid them altogether!

Exercise

Feel alive with 30 minutes of exercise per day!

Keeping active is a key requirement for good health. Your body needs at least 30 minutes of exercise three times per week.

Water

Increase your vitality with 8 glasses of water a day!

Most people need 8 glasses (2 litres/2 quarts) of pure water a day. Tea, coffee, juice, flavoured waters do not count! However a non-caffeinated herbal tea can be an occasional substitute.

Sunshine

Enjoy the rejuvenating benefits of sunshine!

The sun has many healing and rejuvenating properties. You feel so good when you get some sunshine.

Experts believe we need at least 10 minutes of sun on the inside of our arms as a minimum per day!

Air

Breathe deeply to de-stress!

Breathe deeply and slowly. Many people are fast shallow breathers which does not allow your blood to get good oxygen.

Deep breathing will also help to relax you when you are stressed.

Rest

Sleep deeply with 8 hours of rest per night!

Most people generally need 8 hours sleep per night. If you are not waking feeling refreshed and rested you need to get to bed earlier.

Trust

Live in peace with a life full of great relationships!

This is all about the mental and spiritual side of health.

Seek God and enjoy all the blessings He has prepared for your life.

Cookbook Notes

Please read these notes before you start cooking as the recipes will make more sense.

Meals can be prepared using all the meal components in an episode, or you can pick and choose dishes from various episodes.

....

Recipe Preparation

The recipe timing page (at the beginning of each chapter) details the dishes to be prepared, the items and preparation required in your kitchen, and the approximate timings for each part.

Note: Due to other programme components, the "kitchen time" in the Cook:30 programme is recorded in 25 minutes, so the times on the video and in the cookbook will not line up exactly.

Making meals quickly does not happen by accident. Spending 5 minutes getting prepared before starting will save you many more minutes later and make the experience more enjoyable.

Read the recipe ingredients and method completely before beginning. Start with a clear and clean workspace and make sure you have assembled all items you require.

Complicated recipes (usually the main savoury dish) have been divided into different steps. Other simpler recipes generally have all their method and ingredients together.

....

Ingredient Notes

Coconut Milk, Coconut Cream, Cashew Cream

These are used to add creaminess to hot meals.

You can use coconut cream, coconut milk and cashew cream interchangeably. Coconut milk is runnier than coconut cream.

Garlic

I use garlic pressed through a garlic press. Alternatively you can finely chop peeled garlic.

I do not recommend using pre-prepared garlic purees as these just taste awful. Only use fresh garlic.

Ginger/Chilli/Lemongrass Puree

I often use ginger/chilli/lemongrass puree as it adds delicious flavour and is quick to use.

It is available from most supermarkets in tubes or tubs . Alternatively you can make your own by blending ginger/chilli/lemongrass with a little oil and storing in the refrigerator. Or you can peel and finely chop as you go.

Lemon & Lime Juice

Use freshly squeezed. Every lime and lemon varies in the amount of juice it yields so I have included measurements in tablespoons. A rough guide is 2 tablespoons of juice from a small lemon or lime.

Sweeteners/Honey/Date Puree

The recipes do not use added refined sugar. The most convenient natural sweetener is liquid honey which I have used in all recipes requiring sweetening.

Alternatively make up a batch of date puree which is an excellent and inexpensive sweetener.

To make date puree, simply blend equal amounts of dates and water into a smooth puree. This will keep in your refrigerator for a couple of weeks.

There are also other healthy sweeteners available such as apple sauce, agave and maple syrup.

Nuts

All nuts are shelled and raw unless stated.

Cashew nuts are a great creamy nut to use and relatively inexpensive. Cashew pieces (rather than whole) can be used in most dishes and are often half the price.

Oils

My favourite oil is rice bran oil and it is what I use wherever "oil" is used. It is one of the best oils to cook with as it can withstand higher temperatures. It also has a very neutral taste so it is good for dressings. Grape seed and coconut oil are also good. Generally you should not heat olive oil.

Beans, Lentils & Chickpeas

I have used canned beans/chickpeas (garbanzo beans) as this is the most convenient for fast cooking. Drain cans before using.

If you can use freshly cooked beans they will taste better and are significantly cheaper. A 14oz (400g) can of beans is around 2 cups.

I recommend that you soak and cook your own beans and store them in your freezer. You will need to soak overnight in plenty of water. Then cook in fresh water until soft, which will be between 30

minutes and 2 hours, depending on the variety and age. Then freeze them in small containers.

To use, simply defrost by running some hot water over them in a sieve or colander for 30 seconds.

Thickeners: Arrowroot & Cornstarch

I use arrowroot and cornstarch (cornflour) for thickening sauces and desserts in the recipes in this book. Both are interchangeable however you may need to use more when using cornstarch and it may develop a more whiter colour.

Cooking Grains

For grains like brown rice and quinoa I recommend you cook extra and store in your refrigerator for an easy ingredient to use the following few days.

When you cook grains start with boiling water to save time, and return to the boil before turning down to a simmer (just bubbling). Do not stir while cooking and keep the lid on.

Onions

Brown onions are used when not specified however red or white onions can be used instead for most dishes. The onions I generally use for the recipes yield around 1½ cups when chopped.

....

General

Cooking Terms

Saute: to cook food on a high heat and in a little oil while stirring with a wooden spoon.
Simmer: to have food cooking at a low heat setting so it is just bubbling.
Roast: to bake in the oven covered with a little oil. Use fan bake setting to achieve more even cooking.

Mixing

To save dishes, you can mix most recipes in the pot or pan you are cooking in or for salads in your serving bowl.

With salads, mix with your hands if possible. Gently lift up the ingredients and let them fall down with gravity rather than squeezing.

Taste Test

It is difficult to get a recipe that works 100% the same every time, especially when you are using fresh and natural ingredients. Vegetable sizes vary, spices and herbs differ in strength and you can even get differences in evaporation rates with different sized pots.

Make sure you taste test every dish before you serve and be willing to add more seasoning or a little more cooking time if necessary.

Peeling Vegetables

If in good clean condition, I do not peel potatoes, carrots or sweet potato (kumara). You gain extra vitamins, higher yield and save a lot of time.

Quantities

The yield and servings for each dish are an estimate and will vary depending on cooking times and ingredient size.

I have used one cup as an average serving size.

The combined meals in general will feed 4-6 people however this will vary greatly so you will need to determine this.

I usually plan to over cater. I can then fill my fridge with leftovers to last me 1-2 days, or send guests home with lunch for the next day!

Gluten Free & Dairy Free

A large proportion of the recipes are gluten free and all are meat, egg and dairy free. If you have any allergies you will need to check whether each recipe is suitable and make adjustments as required.

....

Kitchen tools

Pots/Pans

I recommend a large non-stick frying pan or cast iron pan to be used for cooking most main dishes. You will also need some medium and small pots (saucepans) and non-stick frying pans. In most cases frying pans and pots can be used interchangeably.

Blenders/Food Processors

Some recipes require a food processor (usually with an S blade). This is generally for non-liquid items.

Smoothies, dressings and pourable recipes require a blender or liquidiser (usually a tall jug with 4 pronged blades). In most cases a stick blender can be used.

Knives

You will need a good sharp knife to make preparation fast, safe and accurate.

Many people end up with 10 cheap $20 knives in their drawer. I recommend just buying 1 good quality (up to $200) chefs knife that will last your lifetime and make your cooking experience more enjoyable.

A lovely combination of colours, flavours and textures that complement one another well.

Spinach, Ginger, Pumpkin & Tofu Curry

Freshly Cooked Quinoa

Revive Raw Salad with Beetroot & Mint

Corn & Pepper Fiesta

Honest Pino Colada

Get ready before you start

Jug	Oven	Counter	Ready on stovetop	Plugged in and ready	Preparation required
Boiling with 3 cups of water	Fan bake 350°F (180°C) Oven tray	Chopping board Sharp chefs knife Serving dishes and glasses	Large frying pan Medium pot	Blender Food processor	2 bananas, peeled, cubed and frozen overnight

Timing

:00	CURRY	Cut pumpkin into cubes and place in oven to roast
:02	QUINOA	Put quinoa on to cook
:04	CURRY	Saute the onion and spices
:07	CORN FIESTA	Assemble all ingredients
:12	CURRY	Blend tomatoes, add more ingredients
:17	SALAD	Process ingredients and combine
:23	CURRY	Add remaining ingredients and stir gently
:26	QUINOA	Plate up and garnish with sliced almonds
:27	PINO COLADA	Add ingredients to blender and finish
:30	FINISH	Serve and enjoy!

Spinach, Ginger, Pumpkin & Tofu Curry

An easy to make hotpot that tastes amazing!
MAKES 8 X 1 CUP SERVES

....

Step 1 – Roast Butternut

2 cups diced butternut pumpkin
1 tablespoon oil

Cut butternut pumpkin into 1in (2cm) cubes. No need to take the skin off.

Put on an oven tray and mix with the oil.

Bake at 350°F (180°C) for around 20 minutes or until soft.

....

Step 2 – Saute Onion

1 large onion diced
2 cloves garlic crushed
1 tablespoon oil
2 tablespoons ginger puree
1 tablespoon ground cumin
1 tablespoon ground turmeric
1 tablespoon ground coriander

In a large frying pan, saute the onion, garlic, oil, ginger until clear.

Add spices and mix well.

....

Step 3 – Add Ingredients

2 x 14oz (400g) cans
crushed tomatoes
2 tablespoons liquid honey
1 teaspoon salt
20oz (600g) pack firm tofu cubed

Add tomatoes to the pan and bring back to the boil.

Add honey, salt and tofu and stir. Let it simmer for several minutes to allow the flavours mingle.

....

Step 4 – Finish & Garnish

2 cups frozen spinach
6fl oz (165ml) coconut milk
garnish: cilantro (fresh coriander)

Remove the butternut pumpkin from the oven and put into pan.

Mix in all remaining ingredients carefully so as not to damage the tofu.

Garnish with roughly chopped cilantro.

....

Revive Raw Salad with Beetroot & Mint

A favourite salad at my cafes – it is on the menu almost all year round!
MAKES 6 X 1 CUP SERVES

1 cup raisins

1 cup boiling water

2 medium beetroot

2 large carrots

½ cup sunflower seeds

10 mint leaves finely sliced

ORANGE DRESSING:

¼ cup freshly squeezed
orange juice

1 tablespoon lemon juice

2 tablespoons liquid honey

½ teaspoon salt

2 tablespoons oil

garnish: mint leaves
garnish: sunflower seeds

Place the raisins and some boiling water in a cup or bowl to soak. After 5 minutes they will be plump and juicy.

Grate the beetroot and carrots by hand or in your food processor using the grater attachment.

In a small bowl or cup mix the orange dressing ingredients.

Drain the water from the raisins.

Combine all ingredients in a serving bowl and mix gently.

Garnish with mint leaves and sunflower seeds.

Freshly Cooked Quinoa

A nutritious light accompaniment for any curry.
MAKES 3 X 1 CUP SERVES

1 cup quinoa

2 cups boiling water

¼ cup sliced almonds

Place quinoa and boiling water in a medium pot with the lid on and bring back to the boil.

Turn down to low and simmer gently (just bubbling) for 12 minutes or until water has been absorbed.

Plate and garnish with sliced almonds.

Tip: Do not stir the quinoa while it is cooking.

Corn & Pepper Fiesta

A delicious accompaniment that goes well with many meals.
MAKES 4 X 1 CUP SERVES

....

2 x 14oz (400g) cans whole kernel sweet corn

1 red bell pepper (capsicum)

4 scallions (spring onions)

1 avocado peeled and cubed

4 tablespoons lime juice

1 teaspoon olive oil

¼ teaspoon salt

Drain liquid from the can and add the corn to a serving bowl.

Finely chop the scallions and bell pepper.

Combine all ingredients in the bowl.

Tip: You can also use fresh or frozen corn for this recipe. Simply run frozen corn under hot water for about 30 seconds to defrost it. The corn kernels do not need to be cooked.

Honest Pino Colada

A healthy take on the classic drink.
MAKES 4 X ¾ CUP SERVES

....

9oz (250g) can pineapple (with own juice, not syrup)
2 bananas, peeled, cubed and frozen overnight
1 tablespoon liquid honey
6fl oz (165ml) coconut milk
garnish: nutmeg powder

Put all ingredients into a blender (or use a stick blender) and blend until smooth.

Pour into glasses and garnish with nutmeg.

Serve immediately.

Tip: If you use non-frozen bananas, put them and the pineapple in the refrigerator before you blend so you have a cold drink.

Instead of shortening your life with dripping pizza, oily fries, and thickshakes. try this healthy combination of fast food alternatives!

Chickpea Pizza

Classic Hummus

Bombay Roasted Potatoes

Cashew & Bell Pepper Dip

Peanut Butter Smoothie

Get ready before you start

Jug	Oven	Counter	Ready on stovetop	Plugged in and ready	Preparation required
	Fan bake 400°F (200°C) 2 oven trays	Chopping board Sharp chefs knife Serving dishes and glasses	Medium frying pan 2 small frying pans	Blender Food processor	2 bananas, peeled, cubed and frozen overnight

Timing

:00	POTATOES	Cut and mix with seasoning, put onto tray and into oven
:03	PIZZA	Mix base, pour onto tray and put in oven
:06	PIZZA	Chop and saute onions, heat tomato sauce
:08	DIP	Chop bell pepper & fry with cashew nuts
:11	HUMMUS	Blend all ingredients and adjust to taste
:15	DIP	Blend ingredients
:17	PIZZA	Arrange toppings on pizza
:21	SMOOTHIE	Blend ingredients and decorate glasses with carob mix
:24	POTATOES	Take out of oven and garnish
:30	FINISH	Serve and enjoy!

Chickpea Pizza

A healthy version and quick to make. You will love the chickpea base!
MAKES 12 PIECES TO SERVE 6 PEOPLE

Step 1 – Make Pizza Base

3 cups chickpea (besan) flour

3 cups water

1 teaspoon onion powder

½ teaspoon garlic powder

1 teaspoon salt

1 tablespoon oil

oil for brushing the tray

In a mixing bowl, combine the chickpea flour with 1 cup of the water and mix well. When mixed, slowly add the rest of the water while mixing. This process will help avoid clumps.

Add the onion powder, garlic powder, salt and oil and mix well.

Select an oven tray (with sides) around 12 x 16in (300 x 400mm). Brush well with oil – especially the corners.

Pour in the chickpea mix and bake at 400°F (200°C) for 15 minutes.

The mixture may seem to be too runny however this is normal.

Step 2 – Saute Onion & Heat Sauce

1 large onion thinly sliced

1 teaspoon oil

2 cups tomato pizza or pasta sauce

In a small frying pan, saute the onion and oil until soft and brown.

Warm up the tomato sauce in a small frying pan

Step 3 – Assemble Pizza Toppings

2 cups baby spinach

½ red bell pepper (capsicum) thinly sliced

½ orange bell pepper (capsicum) thinly sliced

1 cup hummus

12 black olives pitted

On top of the pizza base start with the tomato sauce and then layer on the onion, the spinach and bell peppers.

Place 12 dollops of hummus over the base (4 by 3) and top each with an olive. Cut the pizza base into 12 square pieces.

Tip: This needs to be eaten straight away or the tomato sauce will leak through the base. If you need to eat later – just prepare the ingredients and add the toppings just before serving.

Bombay Roasted Potatoes

A technique to serve roasted potatoes you will love!
MAKES 5 X 1 CUP SERVES

2lb (1kg) white potatoes unpeeled (around 3 large)

2 teaspoons ground turmeric

2 tablespoons oil

1 teaspoon salt

garnish: 4 tablespoons sweet chilli sauce

garnish: ¼ cup finely chopped parsley

Cut the potatoes into 1in (2cm) cubes. Do not peel.

In a bowl combine potatoes with turmeric, oil and salt and mix well.

Place potatoes in an oven tray and bake for 30 minutes at 350°F (180°C). Mix half way through cooking so they cook evenly.

Put the potatoes in a serving bowl.

Drizzle the sweet chilli sauce over the top and garnish with parsley.

Peanut Butter Smoothie

This is a decadent smoothie that kids especially will love. It looks great too!
4 x ¾ CUP SERVES

2 bananas, peeled, cubed and frozen overnight

1 tablespoon peanut butter

1½ cups almond, soy, oat or rice milk

garnish: 3 tablespoons carob powder

Put banana, peanut butter and milk into a blender and blend until smooth. You may need to add some more milk.

In a small bowl, mix the carob powder and water into a runny paste. Drizzle around the inside of the glass with a spoon, twisting the glass as you go.

Pour the smoothie in the glasses and add more carob squiggles on top.

Serve immediately.

Cashew & Bell Pepper Dip

MAKES 2 CUPS

2 red bell peppers (capsicum) roughly chopped

1 tablespoon oil

1 ½ cups cashew nuts

4 cloves garlic

¾ teaspoon salt

2 tablespoons lemon juice

up to 1 cup water

garnish: cashew nut pieces

In a medium frying pan saute the peppers, oil and cashew nuts for around 5 minutes or until the bell peppers are soft.

Combine the pepper mix with the garlic, salt, lemon juice and half the water in a blender. Blend until smooth.

Tip: Every batch is different so you may need to add some or all of the water.

Classic Hummus

MAKES 3 CUPS

2 x 14oz (400g) cans chickpeas (garbanzo beans)

2 tablespoons tahini

½ teaspoon salt

4 tablespoons lemon juice

¼ – ½ cup water

2 cloves garlic

Put all ingredients in a food processor and blend until smooth. You can also use a stick blender or a regular blender however you may have to add more water to keep it flowing.

Taste. Add water/oil/salt as needed. You should be able to taste every ingredient slightly, with not too much of any single ingredient coming through.

Tip: Cook and freeze your own chickpeas. Simply defrost in some hot water.

Corn chowder is usually a soup but this version makes a delicious meal. The 4C salad is very fresh and you will love it!

Corn & Sweet Potato Chowder

Freshly Cooked Brown Rice

4C Salad

Broccoli with a Cheezy Cashew Sauce

Lime & Lemon Spritzer

Get ready before you start

Jug	Oven	Counter	Ready on stovetop	Plugged in and ready	Preparation required
Boiling with 12 cups of water	Fan bake 300°F (150°C) Oven tray	Chopping board Sharp chefs knife Serving dishes and glasses	Large frying pan or pot Medium frying pan 2 medium pots	Blender Food processor with grating attachment	

Timing

:00	RICE	Start brown rice cooking
:02	CHOWDER	Chop onions and start to saute
:04	SALAD	Make 4C mix and put into oven
:07	CHOWDER	Add chopped potato, sweet potato and water to pot and cook
:10	SPRITZER	Combine all ingredients
:12	BROCCOLI	Blend cashew sauce ingredients and commence cooking
:15	CHOWDER	Mash potatoes roughly and add remaining ingredients
:19	SALAD	Grate carrots, add nuts and dressing and plate up
:24	BROCCOLI	Steam broccoli
:26	RICE	Plate and garnish rice
:28	BROCCOLI	Plate up broccoli and drizzle sauce over
:30	FINISH	Serve and enjoy!

Corn & Sweet Potato Chowder

MAKES 6 X 1 CUP SERVES

Step 1 – Saute Onion

1 large onion sliced

1 large red onion cut into chunks

1 tablespoon oil

4 cloves garlic crushed

1 tablespoon chilli puree (optional)

1 teaspoon dried thyme

Saute onions, oil, garlic, chilli, and thyme in a large pot for 5 minutes or until the onion is clear.

1 large red Onion cut into chunks

Step 2 – Cook Potato

4 cups boiling water

1 large potato unpeeled cubes

1 large sweet potato cubes (kumara) unpeeled

Dice the potato and sweet potato into ½in (1cm) squares so they cook quickly.

Add potato, sweet potato and water to the onion mix and cook for around 15 minutes or until soft.

Step 3 – Add Remaining Ingredients

2 cups frozen whole kernel sweet corn

1 stalk celery sliced ½in (1cm)

1 large red bell pepper (capsicum) diced

14oz (400g) can chickpeas (garbanzo beans)

2 tablespoons liquid honey

6fl oz (165ml) coconut cream

1 teaspoon salt

garnish: cilantro (fresh coriander)

With a potato masher mash most of the mix so it thickens, but still retains chunky bits.

Add sweet corn, celery, pepper, chickpeas, and honey and heat so it is nearly bubbling.

Stir in the coconut cream and salt.

Garnish with chopped cilantro

Tip: Fresh or canned whole kernel sweet corn could be used instead of frozen corn in this recipe.

Freshly Cooked Brown Rice

MAKES 6 X 1 CUP SERVES

2 cups long grain brown rice
4 cups boiling water
garnish: Italian parsley

Put the rice and boiling water into a medium pot and put the lid on.

Bring to the boil and turn down to a simmer (just bubbling).

Cook for around 25 minutes or until all the water is gone.

Garnish with chopped parsley.

4C Salad

4C stands for cashew nuts, coconut, carrot and coriander.
This is a very popular salad in my cafes and so easy to make!
MAKES 6 X 1 CUP SERVES

½ cup shredded coconut (unsweetened)

1 cup cashew nuts

2 teaspoons ground coriander

2 tablespoons oil

6 cups grated carrot
(around 4 carrots)

2 tablespoons lemon juice

2 tablespoons olive oil

2 tablespoons liquid honey

1 tablespoon black sesame seeds

garnish: ½ cup chopped cilantro
(fresh coriander)

garnish: shredded coconut

In a mixing bowl combine coconut, cashew nuts, ground coriander and oil and mix.

Pour onto an oven tray and bake at 300°F (150°C) for 10 minutes or until just brown (but not burned).

Grate carrots using the grating attachment in your food processor.

Combine all ingredients in a serving bowl and mix gently.

Garnish with cilantro and shredded coconut.

Broccoli with a Cheezy Cashew Sauce

MAKES 2 CUPS

2 heads broccoli cut into florets

4 cups boiling water

SAUCE:

1 cup cashew nuts

1½ cups water

½ teaspoon salt

¼ teaspoon turmeric powder

1 teaspoon cornstarch (cornflour)

1 tablespoon nutritional yeast flakes

Combine the sauce ingredients in a blender and blend until smooth.

Pour into a medium frying pan and cook for 3 minutes, stirring as it thickens.

Put the broccoli in a medium pot with boiling water and cook for 3 minutes or until tender.

Plate up broccoli and drizzle sauce over.

Lime & Lemon Spritzer

MAKES 4 X 1 CUP SERVES

1 lemon
1 lime
1 quart (1 litre) soda water (sparkling water)
10 mint leaves
8 large ice cubes

Cut lemon in half longways. Set aside one half. Put the other half face down on the chopping board and slice thinly to create "half moons".

Repeat the process above with the lime and add to a jug or carafe.

Take the lemon and lime halves and squeeze their juice into a carafe or jug. Add remaining ingredients.

Tip: Refrigerate if not serving immediately. Serve in transparent tumblers.

I love Indian food! Here is a lovely healthy combination using flavoursome herbs and spices.

Not Butter Chicken Curry

Freshly Cooked Wild Rice

Broccoli, Almond & Cranberry Salad

Cauliflower & Onion Pakoras

Healthy Mango Lassi

Get ready before you start

Jug	Oven	Counter	Ready on stovetop	Plugged in and ready	Preparation required
Boiling with 10 cups of water		Chopping board	Large frying pan	Blender	Pre-freeze 20oz (600g) pack firm tofu and defrost
		Sharp chefs knife	2 medium pots		
		Serving dishes and glasses	Medium frying pan		

Timing

:00	RICE	Put rice on to cook
:02	CURRY	Chop and saute onion mix
:04	PAKORAS	Chop and start to cook cauliflower
:06	SALAD	Chop broccoli and add to cauliflower pot
:08	CURRY	Add remaining ingredients
:12	SALAD	Mix all components
:14	PAKORAS	Make mixture and start cooking
:20	LASSI	Combine ingredients and blend
:24	PAKORAS	Finish cooking and plate
:27	RICE	Plate up and garnish
:29	CURRY	Garnish
:30	FINISH	Serve and enjoy!

Not Butter Chicken Curry

This is a classic Indian dish that usually has chicken, cream and food colouring.
Here is a healthy version that is very popular in my cafes. The frozen tofu gives a nice chewy texture.
MAKES 8 X 1 CUP SERVES

....

Step 1 – Prepare Tofu & Saute Onion

20oz (600g) pack firm tofu frozen

1 large onion diced

1 tablespoon ginger puree

2 cloves garlic crushed

1 tablespoon oil

If your frozen tofu is not defrosted, take it out of the freezer and put it in a bowl with some hot or boiling water so it can defrost.

Saute onions, ginger, garlic and oil in large frying pan for around 5 minutes or until onion is clear.

....

Step 2 – Add Ingredients

1 tablespoon ground cumin

1 tablespoon ground turmeric

1 tablespoon ground coriander

1/8 teaspoon chilli powder

2 x 14oz (400g) cans crushed tomatoes

1 teaspoon salt

2 tablespoons liquid honey

6fl oz (165ml) coconut cream

Add spices and stir while heating to activate flavours.

Add canned tomatoes and mix well.

Slice the defrosted tofu into strips. Squeeze to remove excess water. Add tofu to the pan and gently stir through.

Heat until just bubbling and tofu is evenly heated.

Gently mix through the salt, honey and coconut cream.

....

Step 3 – Garnish

garnish: cilantro (fresh coriander)

Garnish with cilantro.

....

Freshly Cooked Wild Rice

You can buy some lovely rice mixes. Make sure you try some – they are not only tasty but healthy too!
MAKES 6 X 1 CUP SERVES

2 cups wild rice mix
4 cups boiling water
garnish: cilantro (fresh coriander)

Put the rice and boiling water into a medium pot and put the lid on.

Bring to the boil and turn down to a simmer (just bubbling).

Cook for around 25 minutes or until all the water is gone.

Plate up and garnish with chopped cilantro.

Broccoli, Almond & Cranberry Salad

A new delicious way to serve broccoli.
MAKES 5 X 1 CUP SERVES

1 head broccoli cut in florets

3 cups boiling water

1 teaspoon olive oil

¼ teaspoon salt

1 cup dried cranberries

½ cup sliced almonds

Cook the broccoli in boiling water for 4 minutes or until tender.

Drain and rinse in some cold water to stop the cooking process.

Combine all ingredients in a serving bowl.

Cauliflower & Onion Pakoras

MAKES 4 X 1 CUP SERVES

3 cups cauliflower cut into ¼in (½cm) slices

3 cups boiling water

1 large onion sliced into rings

1 cup chickpea (besan) flour

1 cup water

½ teaspoon ground turmeric

1 teaspoon ground coriander

½ teaspoon salt

2 cloves garlic crushed

1 tablespoon liquid honey

2 tablespoons oil for frying

garnish: sweet chilli sauce

garnish: cilantro (fresh coriander)

Slice cauliflower and onion.

Put the cauliflower in a medium pot with boiling water and cook for 5 minutes or until tender.

Measure chickpea flour, spices and salt into a bowl. Add garlic, honey and half the water and mix well.

Add the rest of the water and mix until you have a smooth batter. You may need to add a little more water or flour to get the right consistency.

Place vegetables into the batter and totally cover with the mixture.

Heat a non-stick medium frying pan and put in a splash of oil for each batch.

Fry each side for around 2 minutes or until the batter is cooked and starting to brown.

Plate and squiggle sweet chilli sauce over. Garnish with chopped cilantro.

Healthy Mango Lassi

Frozen mango makes an amazing dessert drink!
MAKES 4 X 1 CUP SERVES

3 cups frozen mango pieces

2 cups almond, soy, oat or rice milk

2 tablespoons liquid honey

2 ripe bananas

garnish: pinch ground nutmeg

Put all ingredients into a blender (or use a stick blender).

Blend until smooth. You may need to add a little more milk to keep the mixture flowing.

Pour into glasses, garnish with nutmeg and serve immediately.

This is a great combination of healthy breakfast favourites. Why not invite friends over for a breakfast or brunch on a Sunday?

Scrambled Tofu with Avocado

Revive Toasted Granola

Homemade Almond Milk

Grilled Veges

Fresh Berries & Mint

Get ready before you start

Jug	Oven	Counter	Ready on stovetop	Plugged in and ready	Preparation required
Boiling with 2 cups of water	Fan bake 300°F (150°C) Baking pan	Chopping board Sharp chefs knife Serving dishes	Large frying pan 2 medium frying pans	Blender	

Timing

:00	MILK	Cover almonds with boiling water
:01	GRANOLA	Mix granola grains, seeds and nuts and put in oven
:06	TOFU	Mix everything and put in a pan to start cooking
:10	VEGES	Chop and grill veges – leave in pan to keep warm
:14	MILK	Blend almond milk and put in fridge to cool
:17	GRANOLA	Remove from oven and put in fridge to cool
:18	TOFU	Plate up tofu and add avocado
:20	VEGES	Plate up and add parsley
:22	BERRIES	Turn chopping board over, prepare berries, plate and garnish
:27	TOFU	Plate up scrambled tofu and add chopped herbs
:29	GRANOLA	Add dried fruit and plate up
:30	FINISH	Serve and enjoy!

Scrambled Tofu with Avocado

A lovely flavoursome alternative to scrambled eggs. You will not believe how good it tastes!
MAKES 3 X 1 CUP SERVES

....

Step 1 – Saute Onion & Add Ingredients

½ red onion finely sliced
(half moons)

1 tablespoon oil

2 teaspoons ginger puree

2 cloves garlic crushed

10oz (300g) firm tofu crumbled

¼ teaspoon ground turmeric

2 tablespoons soy sauce
or tamari

In a medium frying pan, saute the onion, oil, ginger and garlic.

WIth your hands crumble the tofu on top of the onions and continue to cook for around 3-5 minutes or until onion is clear.

Add remaining ingredients to pan and mix and continue to cook for around 5 minutes, stirring regularly.

....

Step 2 – Garnish

1 avocado

garnish: cilantro (fresh coriander)

garnish: 1 tablespoon liquid honey

garnish: 1 tablespoon lime juice

Put the scrambled tofu into your serving dish.

Dice avocado, chop cilantro and sprinkle over the tofu.

Drizzle the honey and lime juice on top.

....

Grilled Veges

A lovely medley of colours and flavours.
SERVES 4

....

1 tablespoon oil
30 small button mushrooms
4 large tomatoes
2 zucchini (courgette)
½ teaspoon salt
garnish: parsley

Wash the mushrooms and cut in half. Make random cuts in the zucchini so they are all similar sizes. Cut the tomatoes in half.

In a medium frying pan saute the tomato and mushrooms with 2 teaspoons of the oil for around 5 minutes or until getting soft.

In another medium frying pan saute the zucchini with 1 teaspoon of oil for around 5 minutes.

Shake and turn as required.

Sprinkle with salt. Plate and garnish with parsley.

Revive Toasted Granola

A healthy crunchy granola that is far better for you than most packaged breakfast cereals.
MAKES 4 CUPS

1 cup regular rolled oats
1 cup quick oats (fine rolled oats)
3 tablespoons cashew nut pieces
½ cup shredded coconut
½ cup sliced almonds
4 tablespoons sesame seeds
3 tablespoons oil
3 tablespoons liquid honey
½ cup sunflower seeds
½ cup dried raisins
½ cup dried cranberries

Mix oats, nuts and seeds in a large baking pan.

Pour the honey and oil over and mix well.

Bake at 300°F (150°C) for 20 minutes or until golden. Stir the mixture half way through so it cooks evenly.

Pour granola into serving bowl and let it cool in the fridge.

Shortly before serving mix in the dried fruit.

Tip: This will store in an airtight container in your pantry for up to several weeks.

Tip: I use a mixture of regular rolled oats and quick oats for a more interesting texture. However you can use either if you do not have both.

Tip: Other dried fruits can be used such as apricots and dates.

Fresh Berries & Mint

I love berries and they are a great fresh addition to breakfast.
MAKES 3 CUPS

1 cup fresh strawberries

2 cups fresh blueberries

garnish: mint

Cut green tops off the strawberries then chop into quarters.

Pour blueberries into a serving bowl.

Add chopped strawberries and gently mix.

Garnish with finely chopped mint.

Homemade Almond Milk

A healthy milk alternative you can make at home!
MAKES 5 CUPS

2 cups boiling water

¾ cup whole almonds

4 cups filtered water

5 dried dates

1 pinch salt

1 drop vanilla essence (optional)

Soak almonds in a bowl with boiling water for 10 minutes to soften. Drain.

Put all ingredients into a blender. A food processor or stick blender may suffice, but will not produce such a creamy milk.

Blend for around 2 minutes or until creamy. Use as high a speed as possible. You want creamy milk, not water and small pieces of almonds.

Tip: You can use straight away or you can store in the fridge for up to 3 days. You will have to stir or shake each time you use it as the ingredients will separate.

Tip: You can pour through a sieve to get a more consistent milk without almond "flecks".

You will love these
filos and the two
lovely salads in
this meal!

Tuscan Butternut & Spinach Filo Parcels

Mesclun Mango Salad

Fresh Pesto Vegetable Mingle

Classic Strawberry Smoothie

Get ready before you start

Jug	Oven	Counter	Ready on stovetop	Plugged in and ready	Preparation required
Boiling with 6 cups of water	Fan bake 350°F (180°C) Oven tray	Chopping board Sharp chefs knife Serving dishes and glasses	Medium frying pan Medium pot	Blender Food processor	

Timing

:00	PARCELS	Roast butternut, saute onions and garlic
:05	MINGLE	Cut carrots, cauliflower and broccoli and cook in boiling water
:09	MINGLE	Blend Pesto ingredients
:12	MINGLE	Drain and rinse with cold water to stop cooking
:13	PARCELS	Make butternut mixture and fold filo triangles
:20	SALAD	Combine all ingredients
:24	MINGLE	Combine with pesto and plate up
:26	SMOOTHIE	Put ingredients into blender and blend
:29	PARCELS	Plate up filo parcels and garnish
:30	FINISH	Serve and enjoy!

Tuscan Butternut & Spinach Filo Parcels

MAKES 8 PARCELS

Step 1 – Cook Butternut & Saute Onion

2 cups butternut pumpkin diced

1 teaspoon oil (for butternut)

1 tablespoon cumin powder

1 onion finely diced

1 clove garlic crushed

1 teaspoon oil (for onion)

Mix the diced pumpkin with 1 teaspoon of oil on an oven tray. Sprinkle the cumin over the top. Bake for around 15 minutes at 350°F (180°C) or until soft.

In a frying pan saute the onion, garlic and 1 teaspoon oil for 5 minutes or until soft.

Step 2 – Assemble Filling

1 cup dried cranberries

1 cup frozen spinach defrosted – around 13oz (360g)

14oz (400g) can black-eyed peas drained

½ teaspoon salt

16 sheets filo pastry – size around 12x8in (30x20cm)

oil for brushing

Defrost the spinach using hot water. Squeeze to remove the water.

In a mixing bowl combine pumpkin with onion, cranberries, spinach black-eyed peas and salt. Mix and mash slightly with a fork.

Put 4 sheets of filo pastry onto your chopping board on top of each other. Cut in half lengthwise so you have 2 long strips to make 2 parcels.

The filo dries out fast, so work quickly and cover any not in use.

Spoon ½ cup of the mix onto the bottom right corner. Fold into a triangle. Keep folding over into triangles until you have used all the pastry. There will be around 4–5 folds required depending on the size.

Repeat for each filo. Put the parcels onto a lightly oiled oven tray.

Step 3 – Cook & Garnish

garnish: 1 teaspoon black sesame seeds

garnish: 1 teaspoon white sesame seeds

garnish: cilantro (fresh coriander)

Using a brush, oil the filo parcels lightly. You can also use an oil spray. Make sure the tops and sides are covered as these burn the easiest.

Place on an oven tray and sprinkle with the sesame seeds.

Bake in the oven at 350°F (180°C) for around 10 minutes or until crunchy.

Garnish with cilantro.

Fresh Pesto Vegetable Mingle

MAKES 6 X 1 CUP SERVES

2 cups carrots sliced
2 cups cauliflower
2 cups broccoli
6 cups boiling water
1 cup Homemade Basil Pesto
garnish: cashew nuts
garnish: basil

Put boiling water in a medium pot on the stove.

Slice carrots diagonally and put into pot.

Cut cauliflower into bite-sized florets and add to pot.

Cut broccoli into bite-sized florets and put into pot.

Cook for around 3 minutes from when the broccoli is added or until all vegetables are tender.

Drain and immediately rinse with cold water to stop the cooking.

In your serving bowl combine vegetables with pesto and garnish with cashew nuts and sliced basil leaves.

Homemade Basil Pesto

MAKES 2 CUPS

1 large bunch fresh basil
(around 4oz/100g)
1 cup cashew nuts
¼ cup oil
½ teaspoon salt
¼ cup lemon juice (2–3 lemons)
2 cloves garlic

Put all ingredients into a blender and blend until it is well mixed, but there are still some nut pieces showing.

Tip: For a different flavour you can use almonds, pine nuts or walnuts instead of cashew nuts.

Mesclun Mango Salad

MAKES 6 X 1 CUP SERVES

3oz (100g) mesclun lettuce mix or baby spinach

1 mango

½ cup sliced almonds

1 tablespoon lime juice

Rinse the mesclun in a little water to liven it up. Drain well.

Peel the mango, cut off 2 large "cheeks", slice off the flesh and cut into strips.

Combine all ingredients in a serving bowl and mix gently.

Tip: Mesclun is a salad mix of assorted small, young salad leaves. Traditionally specific lettuces were used in equal portions however many other leafy vegetables, such as spinach and arugula are now included.

Classic Strawberry Smoothie

MAKES 4 X ¾ CUP SERVES

....

3 ripe bananas

1½ cups almond, soy, oat or rice milk

1 tablespoon liquid honey

1½ cups frozen strawberries

Place all ingredients in a blender (or use a stick blender).

Pour into serving glasses and garnish with shredded coconut.

Serve immediately.

Episode
7

This is a tasty and healthy Mexican meal you can make at home for your family. I love meals where I can mix and match different components.

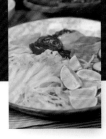

Revive Chilli on Corn Chips

Fresh Toppings

Healthy Cheezy Cashew Sauce

Pan Fried Vegetables

Blueberry "Better Than Ice Cream"

Get ready before you start

Jug	Oven	Counter	Ready on stovetop	Plugged in and ready	Preparation required
		Chopping board	Large frying pan	Blender	
		Sharp chefs knife	2 medium frying pans	Food processor	
		Serving dishes			

Timing

:00	CHILLI	Saute onions
:04	VEGETABLES	Chop and saute
:10	SAUCE	Blend ingredients and cook
:15	TOPPINGS	Cut up tomatoes, lettuce, red onion and avocado
:20	ICE CREAM	Blend ingredients, put into glasses and put in freezer
:25	CHILLI	Add remaining ingredients and garnish
:27	CORN CHIPS	Put into a bowl
:28	VEGETABLES	Put into serving dish
:29	SAUCE	Pour into a bowl
:30	FINISH	Serve and enjoy!

Revive Chilli on Corn Chips

This is a delicious chilli that is so easy to make. Make it as mild or hot as you like.
MAKES 8 X 1 CUP SERVES

Step 1 – Saute Onion & Add Ingredients

1 large onion diced

1 tablespoon oil

1 tablespoon ginger puree

2 cloves garlic crushed

1 teaspoon cajun spice powder

1 pinch cayenne pepper diced

1 large red bell pepper (capsicum) finely diced

2 x 14oz (400g) cans crushed tomatoes

14oz (400g) can black beans

14oz (400g) can red kidney beans

In a large frying pan saute the onion, oil, ginger and garlic until the onion is clear.

Add spices and stir while heating to release their flavours.

Add bell pepper and canned tomatoes and stir through.

Drain the canned beans and add to the pan.

Simmer on low heat stirring occasionally.

Step 2 – Finish & Garnish

6fl oz (160ml) coconut cream

1 tablespoon liquid honey

1 teaspoon salt

1 cup frozen whole kernel sweet corn

garnish: cilantro (fresh coriander)

corn chips

Add remaining ingredients and bring up to temperature.

Garnish with chopped cilantro.

Serve with corn chips.

Fresh Toppings

Colourful fresh vegetables.

....

½ medium iceburg lettuce

4 tomatoes sliced (use both red and yellow for colour if available)

1 avocado sliced and fanned

½ small telegraph cucumber sliced

2 limes quartered

Prepare vegetables and lay out on a large serving platter. Arrange in colour groups for the best presentation.

Healthy Cheezy Cashew Sauce

A lovely healthy alternative to cheese sauce!
MAKES 2 CUPS

....

1 cup cashew nuts
1 teaspoon cornstarch (cornflour)
¼ teaspoon turmeric powder
¼ teaspoon salt
1 tablespoon nutritional yeast flakes
1½ cups water

Combine all ingredients in a blender and blend until smooth.

Pour into medium frying pan and heat while stirring for around 3–5 minutes or until it thickens to the desired consistency.

Tip: For a cheezier sauce add more yeast flakes.

Pan Fried Vegetables

MAKES 2 CUPS

1 red onion

1 red bell pepper (capsicum)

1 orange bell pepper (capsicum)

1 green bell pepper (capsicum)

1 tablespoon oil

½ teaspoon salt

Slice onion and bell peppers and lightly fry in a medium frying pan with oil and salt.

Do not overcook – they should retain their shape and have a little crunch.

Blueberry "Better Than Ice Cream"

SERVES 4

¾ cup cashew nuts

½ cup water

2 cups frozen blueberries

2 tablespoons liquid honey

10 large mint leaves

2 bananas peeled, cubed and frozen overnight (optional)

garnish: sliced almonds

garnish: mint

Ideally you will need a food processor for this recipe (not a blender as they are for liquids).

Blend cashew nuts with ½ cup of water to form a smooth paste.

Add the rest of the ingredients and process until smooth.

You may need to add more water to keep the mixture smooth but only add just enough as you do not want it to become a smoothie!

Store in the freezer until just before serving. Do not freeze for more than 20 minutes or it will freeze into a block.

Pour into serving dishes. Garnish with sliced almonds and mint.

Everyone loves
a satay! Here are
some popular Thai
dishes I serve at
my cafes.

Thai Chickpea Satay

Sunflower Cream

Pad Thai Noodles

Asian Salad with Ginger

Apricot Bliss Balls

Get ready before you start

Jug	Oven	Counter	Ready on stovetop	Plugged in and ready	Preparation required
Boiling with 8 cups of water		Chopping board Sharp chefs knife Serving dishes	Large frying pan	Blender Food processor	

Timing

:00	BALLS	Soak fruit and nuts in water
01	SATAY	Chop onions and saute
:03	NOODLES	Pour boiling water over noodles, cover and leave to cook
:05	SATAY	Add further ingredients and leave to simmer
:10	CREAM	Blend ingredients
:13	SALAD	Combine all ingredients together
:17	BALLS	Drain fruit and nuts, blend and make balls
:23	NOODLES	Drain noodles and mix all ingredients
:28	SATAY	Stir in coconut cream and garnish
:30	FINISH	Serve and enjoy!

Thai Chickpea Satay

These Thai spices, ginger and peanuts combine together very well!
MAKES 8 X 1 CUP SERVES

Step 1 – Saute Onion

1 large onion chopped

2 cloves garlic crushed

4 tablespoons ginger puree

2 tablespoons oil

In a large frying pan saute the onion, garlic, ginger and oil until onion is clear.

Step 2 – Add Ingredients

1 pinch cayenne pepper

1 teaspoon ground turmeric

1 teaspoon ground cumin

½ cup peanut butter

½ cup water

2 x 14oz (400ml) cans crushed tomatoes

2 x 14oz (400g) cans chickpeas (garbanzo beans)

1 teaspoon salt

3 tablespoons liquid honey

Stir in spices and stir for around 30 seconds to activate the flavours.

Mix peanut butter and water in a cup to make a pourable paste and add to pan.

Add tomatoes, chickpeas, salt and honey and heat until it is just bubbling.

Step 3 – Finish & Garnish

6fl oz (165ml) coconut cream

garnish: cilantro (fresh coriander)

Turn off heat and stir in coconut cream.

Garnish with chopped cilantro.

Pad Thai Noodles

MAKES 6 X 1 CUP SERVES

9oz (250g) ¼in (5mm) rice noodles

5 cups boiling water

½ teaspoon salt

2 tablespoons liquid honey

2 tablespoons sweet chilli sauce

2 tablespoons soy sauce or tamari

1 tablespoon sesame oil

6 small scallions (spring onions)

½ red bell pepper (capsicum) finely diced

1 ½ tablespoons finely chopped lemongrass

garnish: ½ cup finely chopped roasted and salted peanuts

garnish: cilantro (fresh coriander) roughly chopped

garnish: 2 limes quartered

Put noodles in a mixing bowl.

Cover with boiling water and put a plate on top.

Sit for around 5–12 minutes (every noodle is different) or until soft.

Drain in a colander, put noodles back into the bowl.

Add remaining ingredients and mix gently.

Plate and garnish with peanuts, cilantro and lime quarters.

Sunflower Cream

A tasty healthy alternative to sour cream.
MAKES 1 CUP

¾ cup water

1 cup sunflower seeds

¼ cup lemon juice

1 teaspoon onion powder

½ teaspoon salt

Combine all ingredients in a blender.

Blend well until smooth.

You may have to add a little more water so the blender keeps everything turning. However only add a little bit at a time as it can easily get too runny.

Pour into serving bowl.

Tip: This will not keep well so use the same day.

Asian Salad with Ginger

MAKES 4 X 1 CUP SERVES

2 cups bok choy sliced into strips
(around 2 heads)

4 small carrots cut into matchsticks

½ red bell pepper (capsicum) sliced

2 tablespoons sesame oil

¼ teaspoon salt

½ cup pickled ginger

garnish: 1 teaspoon white
sesame seeds

garnish: 1 teaspoon black
sesame seeds

Prepare vegetables.

Combine all ingredients in a serving bowl.

Tip: You can use other fresh leafy greens (like baby spinach) in this salad.

Apricot Bliss Balls

MAKES 25 BALLS

1 cup dried dates
1 cup dried apricots
½ cup cashew nuts
½ cup walnuts
½ cup sunflower seeds
½ cup almonds
3 cups boiling water
garnish: ½ cup shredded coconut

Measure fruit, nuts and seeds into a mixing bowl and cover with boiling water. Leave to soften for 15 minutes.

Drain. Put softened fruit, nuts and seeds in a food processor and blend until it all clumps up.

Spoon 2 tablespoons of the mixture into your hand and roll into small balls.

Gently toss in a bowl with the coconut.

A delicious
combination of
four popular salads
in my cafes!

French Puy Lentils & Roasted Beetroot

Spanish Smoked Rice with Peanuts

Fresh Cos Caesar Salad with Croutons

Thai Green Curry Mingle

Sparkling Fruity Punch

Get ready before you start

Jug	Oven	Counter	Ready on stovetop	Plugged in and ready	Preparation required
Boiling with 4 cups of water	Fan bake 350°F (180°C) 2 oven trays	Chopping board Sharp chefs knife Serving dishes and glasses	Medium pot Medium frying pan	Blender	3 cups of cooked long grain brown rice 3 cups cooked lentils

Timing

:00	LENTILS	Cut beetroot and put in oven
:02	MINGLE	Cut sweet potato and put in oven
:04	MINGLE	Cut cauliflower and broccoli and put on stove to cook
:06	COS	Blend Tahini Dressing ingredients
:08	MINGLE	Drain cauliflower and broccoli and rinse in cold water
:10	COS	Cut croutons and put in oven
:12	RICE	Combine all ingredients and garnish
:16	PUNCH	Combine ingredients in a jug
:18	MINGLE	Add remaining ingredients and garnish
:22	COS	Prepare remaining ingredients and plate up
:25	LENTIL	Add remaining ingredients and garnish
:30	FINISH	Serve and enjoy!

French Puy Lentils & Roasted Beetroot

MAKES 6 X 1 CUP SERVES

Step 1 – Chop & Roast Beetroot

2 large beetroot

1 tablespoon oil

1 tablespoon ground clove powder

Chop beetroot into ½in (1cm) cubes.

Put onto an oven tray and mix with oil and clove powder and bake at 350°F (180°C) for around 25 minutes.

Step 2 – Combine Ingredients

3 cups (or 2 x 14oz (400g) cans) cooked French green lentils (Puy lentils)

1 yellow bell pepper (capsicum) diced

1 tablespoon whole-grain (seeded) mustard

2 tablespoons sweet chilli sauce

½ teaspoon salt

2 tablespoons lemon juice

1 clove garlic crushed

2 teaspoons liquid honey

1 teaspoon olive oil

garnish: mint

Remove the beetroot from the oven and place in a large mixing bowl.

Add remaining ingredients to the bowl and combine gently.

Pour into a serving bowl and garnish with chopped mint.

Tip: Brown lentils can be used as an alternative to French green lentils (Puy lentils) although they don't hold together as well once cooked. I cook a large batch of lentils and freeze in containers for later use. When needed I defrost them in hot water. Canned lentils could also be used in this recipe.

Spanish Smoked Rice with Peanuts

This is a great salad to make if you have leftover rice.
MAKES 6 X 1 CUP SERVES

3 cups cooked long grain brown rice

1 cup frozen peas

½ cup Tahini Dressing (see next page)

2 teaspoons smoked paprika

1 teaspoon salt

1 tablespoon sweet chilli sauce

½ cup roasted peanuts

1 red bell pepper (capsicum) finely diced

1 cup cherry tomatoes halved

garnish: Italian parsley

Combine all ingredients in a serving bowl and mix gently.

Tip: I find that the strength of smoked paprika varies considerably between batches and brands so taste first as you may need to add a little more.

Tip: If you do not have pre-cooked rice available, you can cook your own by combining 1 cup rice and 2 cups boiling water in a pot and simmering for 20 minutes with the lid on.

Fresh Cos Caesar Salad with Croutons

MAKES 8 X 1 CUP SERVES

3 slices thick wholemeal bread

2 tablespoons oil

½ teaspoon salt

1 medium romaine (cos) lettuce

½ cup sundried tomatoes sliced

1 avocado cubed ½in (1cm)

¼ cup Tahini Dressing

Cut the bread into cubes, mix with oil and salt. Put into a medium frying pan and heat gently for 10 minutes or until just crisp. Toss regularly. Allow to cool before using.

Cut off the core and place the lettuce leaves on a platter.

Scatter the croutons, sundried tomato, and avocado over the lettuce.

Drizzle the tahini dressing over the top.

Tahini Dressing

A healthy alternative to aioli or mayonnaise.
MAKES 1½ CUPS

10 tablespoons tahini

1 tablespoon liquid honey

2 tablespoons lemon juice

½ teaspoon salt

1 large clove garlic

8 tablespoons water

Put all ingredients in a blender and blend.

You may need to add more water to achieve a pourable consistency.

Tip: This version requires a blender as it contains garlic. If you don't want to use a blender, crush the garlic and just stir ingredients well.

Thai Green Curry Mingle

MAKES 6 X 1 CUP SERVES

2 large sweet potato (kumara)
2 tablespoons oil
¼ head cauliflower
1 head broccoli
4 cups boiling water
1 red bell pepper (capsicum)
1 teaspoon Thai green curry paste
¼ cup water
2 tablespoons lemongrass puree
½ teaspoon salt
3oz (100g) can bamboo shoots
2 tablespoons liquid honey
½ cup Tahini Dressing
(see previous page)
garnish: cilantro (fresh coriander)

Cut sweet potato into 1in (2cm) cubes and mix with oil spread on an oven tray.

Roast for 15 minutes at 350°F (180°C) or until soft.

Cut cauliflower and broccoli into florets. Put in a medium pot with boiling water and cook for 2 minutes.

Cut bell pepper into thin slices.

Put all vegetables in serving bowl.

In a cup mix the green curry paste, water and lemongrass puree together to form a runny paste. Pour over vegetables.

Add salt, bamboo shoots, honey and Tahini Dressing and mix gently with your hands.

Garnish with cilantro.

Sparkling Fruity Punch

This is an excellent healthy drink for festive occasions.
MAKES 4 X 1 CUP SERVES

....

1 quart (1 litre) orange juice
½ cup diced strawberries
2 limes (1 juiced, 1 sliced)
2 lemons (1 juiced, 1 sliced)
4 tablespoons finely chopped mint
2 cups soda water /spritzer water
ice

Put orange juice, strawberries into a serving jug.

Juice 1 lime and 1 lemon and add.

Cut 1 lemon and 1 lime into half moons and add.

Add the mint.

Just before serving add the soda water and ice.

You will love this combination of fresh Asian dishes. And they are so easy to make!

Asian Peanut Stir Fry

Honey Glazed Tofu

Asian Sesame Greens Salad

Edamame

Sliced Pineapple with Mint & Lime Juice

Get ready before you start

Jug	Oven	Counter	Ready on stovetop	Plugged in and ready	Preparation required
Boiling with 3 cups of water		Chopping board Sharp chefs knife Serving dishes	Large frying pan Medium frying pan		2 cups of cooked long grain brown rice needed

Timing

:00	STIR FRY	Chop onions and start to saute, soak raisins
:04	TOFU	Start tofu cooking and make marinade
:08	SALAD	Cut vegetables, assemble and add dressing
:12	EDAMAME	Put in boiling water
:14	STIR FRY	Add further ingredients to the pan
:20	TOFU	Pour marinade over the tofu, plate up and garnish
:23	PINEAPPLE	Cut pineapple slices, squeeze lime juice over and garnish
:27	STIR FRY	Add garnishes
:29	EDAMAME	Drain, add oil and salt and plate up
:30	FINISH	Serve and enjoy!

Asian Peanut Stir Fry

This is a delicious stir fry! I love dishes where you just keep adding flavourful ingredients to the pan!
MAKES 6 X 1 CUP SERVES

Step 1 – Saute Vegetables

1 large red onion sliced
2 tablespoons oil
1 red bell pepper (capsicum) diced
1 large zucchini (courgette) diced
2 tablespoons ginger puree
2 cloves garlic crushed
1 cup raisins
1 cup boiling water

In a large pan saute the onion, oil, bell pepper, zucchini, ginger and garlic for 5 minutes until they start to soften.

Put raisins into a small bowl with boiling water and set aside to plumpen.

Step 2 – Add Ingredients

2 tablespoons peanut butter
4 tablespoons water
2 tablespoons liquid honey
2 tablespoons soy sauce or tamari
2 scallions (spring onions) sliced
1 cup peanuts roasted
2 cups cooked long grain brown rice
½ teaspoon salt
juice of 2 limes

In a cup mix the peanut butter with the water to form a pourable paste. Pour over the vegetables and stir through.

Add honey, soy sauce, scallions, peanuts and rice and stir for 5 minutes or until heated.

Drain the raisins, add and stir through.

Squeeze the lime juice over the top.

Step 3 – Garnish

garnish: mint
garnish: cilantro (fresh coriander)
garnish: ½ cup chopped peanuts
garnish: 2 limes quartered

Finely chop the fresh herbs and sprinkle over.

Scatter the chopped peanuts on top and add lime wedges.

Honey Glazed Tofu

Tofu soaks up all these lovely Asian flavours.
MAKES 4-8 SERVES

1 tablespoon oil

10oz (300g) pack firm tofu

4 tablespoons liquid honey

2 tablespoons soy sauce or tamari

1 tablespoon lemon juice

2 tablespoons ginger puree

4 tablespoons warm water

garnish: white sesame seeds

garnish: black sesame seeds

garnish: liquid honey

Heat a medium non-stick frying pan and coat with oil.

Cut the tofu into slabs around ½ in (1cm) thick.

Cook the tofu strips on high heat for around 5 minutes each side - they should firm up a little and darken slightly. This may take a little longer depending on how much water is in your tofu.

In a bowl mix together the marinade of honey, soy sauce, lemon juice, ginger and water and pour over the tofu, ensuring it is coated evenly.

Cook for around 3 minutes per side or until they turn golden brown. Ideally the liquid should just be drying out as you finish cooking.

Arrange on a platter and garnish with sesame seeds and drizzle with honey.

Tip: Heating the tofu before adding flavoursome ingredients is the best way to infuse flavour into tofu because the heat draws the flavour in.

Sliced Pineapple with Mint & Lime Juice

Fresh, simple and tasty!
SERVES 4

1 pineapple
10 mint leaves finely sliced
2 tablespoons lime juice
garnish: 1 lime cut into wedges

Cut skin off the pineapple, cut into quarters longways and cut out core. Cut into ½in (1cm) strips. Fan out and arrange on a platter.

Sprinkle finely chopped mint leaves and the lime juice over top.

Garnish with lime wedges.

Asian Sesame Greens Salad

You will never believe how this simple "dressing" can make these greens taste so good!
MAKES 10 X 1 CUP SERVES

6 cups fresh greens
- 2 pressed cups spinach
- 2 pressed cups bok-choy
- 2 pressed cups choy-sum
1 red bell pepper (capsicum)
2 tablespoons liquid honey
1-2 tablespoons sesame oil
2 tablespoons white sesame seeds
2 tablespoons black sesame seeds

Chop the green vegetables into 1½in (3cm) strips. Cut across the stalks so you break up the stringy texture.

Slice the bell pepper into thin strips.

Mix vegetables in a bowl and drizzle the honey and sesame oil over the top and mix gently. Sprinkle the sesame seeds on top.

Tip: The salad greens used here are only an example combination, choose whatever varieties you have available.

Edamame

So quick and delicious. Eating these is a fun and slightly addictive experience! Simply take one edamame pod and put it in your mouth while holding the end with your fingers. Then slide the beans out with your teeth and discard the pod.

7oz (200g) frozen pre-cooked edamame
(soy beans with pods)
2 cups boiling water
¼ teaspoon salt
1 teaspoon virgin olive oil

Put edamame in a pot of boiling water for 15 minutes.

If the edamame are not pre-cooked, leave for another 5 minutes.

Drain and put into your serving bowl and toss with salt and olive oil.

After you have made these corn fritters once they will become one of your favourite quick meals!

Curried Indian Zucchini Fritters

Revivedorf Salad with Tofu Mayo

Pineapple & Mint Salsa

Plum & Ginger Oat Slice

Get ready before you start

Jug	Oven	Counter	Ready on stovetop	Plugged in and ready	Preparation required
	Fan bake 350°F (180°C)	Chopping board	Large frying pan	Blender or stick blender	
	Oven dish	Sharp chefs knife			
		Serving dishes			

Timing

:00	SLICE	Make oat mix, de-stone plums, make slice and put in oven
:07	FRITTERS	Saute onion, grate zucchini, make mixture, start first batch cooking
:15	SALSA	Mix all ingredients
:18	FRITTERS	Turn first batch
:19	SALAD	Put Tofu Mayo ingredients into blender
:22	FRITTERS	Remove first batch, put on second batch, attend to as required
:24	SALAD	Combine ingredients and dressing
:28	FRITTERS	Plate up and garnish
:29	SLICE	Remove from oven, slice and plate
:30	FINISH	Serve and enjoy!

Curried Indian Zucchini Fritters

When you find out how easy these are to make you will make them all the time!
MAKES 20 SMALL OR 10 LARGE FRITTERS

....

Step 1 – Saute Onion & Add Spices

1 medium onion finely diced

1 teaspoon oil

3 zucchini (courgette)

½ cup water (optional)

2 tablespoons sweet chilli sauce

1 tablespoon black sesame seeds

1 teaspoon mild curry powder

2 cups chickpea (besan) flour

½ teaspoon salt

½ cup cilantro (fresh coriander)

In a large non-stick frying pan saute the onion and oil until the onion is clear.

Grate the zucchini with a hand grater using the largest holes.

Mix all the ingredients together in a mixing bowl. The moisture from the zucchini should make everything the right consistency however you may need to add up to half a cup of water.

....

Step 2 – Fry Fritters & Garnish

oil for shallow frying

garnish: sweet chilli sauce, salsa or chutney

garnish: cilantro (fresh coriander)

Add the oil to the same pan and bring up to temperature. Spoon the fritter mix into the pan and let it spread out to form fritters. You may need to push the mix down and/or coax it into shape.

Cook for around 4-5 minutes each side or until golden brown and cooked right through.

Serve on a platter with sweet chilli sauce, salsa or chutney on the side or drizzled over the top.

Garnish with chopped cilantro.

Tip: You can substitute wholemeal flour for the chickpea flour in this recipe.

Tip: When making fritters I make a test one first to check flavour, the heat of the pan and that everything sticks together.

....

Revivedorf Salad

Fresh, alive and full of crunch.
MAKES 6 X 1 CUP SERVES

2 large red apples

2 big stalks celery

½ cup tofu mayo

1½oz (50g) (2-3 cups)
baby spinach or other greens

1 tablespoon lemon juice

½ cup walnuts (optional)

Core and chop apples into 1in (2cm) cubes.

Slice celery into ½in (1cm) pieces.

Mix all ingredients in a serving bowl.

Tip: The apple will oxidise (go brown) quickly so you need to prepare this salad close to serving time. Ensure you dress the apples quickly as this will help stop them going brown.

Tofu Mayo

A healthy lower fat alternative to mayonnaise or aioli.
MAKES 2 CUPS

2 cups (12oz/350g) firm tofu

1 tablespoon whole-grain (seeded) mustard

5 tablespoons lemon juice

1 tablespoon liquid honey

1 teaspoon salt

1 clove garlic

Put all ingredients into a blender and blend until smooth.

You may need to add a little more water to get the right consistency.

Tip: You can add a little turmeric if you want a yellow colour.

Pineapple & Mint Salsa

A quick, easy and tasty addition to any meal.
MAKES 2 CUPS

....

½ small red onion finely chopped

½ red bell pepper (capsicum) finely chopped

1 small bunch of mint finely chopped

17oz (500g) can crushed pineapple (in own juice) drained

3 tablespoons lemon juice

sprinkle of cayenne pepper (optional)

Finely chop onion, bell pepper and mint.

Combine all ingredients in a serving bowl.

Tip: This salsa is best made fresh. It does not taste the same the next day.

Plum & Ginger Oat Slice

Lovely healthy sweet option. This recipe is versatile – try other canned fruit like apricots, apples or peaches.
MAKES 8 LARGE SLABS OR 16 SMALL SLABS

3 cups quick oats (fine rolled oats)

½ cup sesame seeds

½ cup ground almonds

¼ cup sliced almonds

½ cup shredded coconut

4 tablespoons oil

¾ cup liquid honey

2 teaspoons ginger puree

3 x 14oz (400g) can black plums (about 3 cups/12 plums)

garnish: sliced almonds (optional)

Mix all dry ingredients together in a large mixing bowl.

Add the oil, honey and ginger and mix well.

Select a oven dish approximately 8x12in (20x30cm) and brush lightly with oil.

Firmly press half the mixture into the oven dish.

Drain the plums well and take out any stones. Crush with your fingers, place on top of the oat base and press down.

Sprinkle the remaining oat mix evenly on top of the plums and press down evenly. Spray or brush a little oil on top to prevent it burning.

Bake for 25 minutes at 350°F (180°C) or until golden brown.

Cool and cut into slabs with a serrated knife.

This is a delicious meal using Thai flavours. Use plenty of ginger, cilantro and lime juice.

Thai Red Curry with Chickpeas

Rice Noodles with Cilantro & Lime Juice

Thai Ginger Coleslaw

Sticky Rice Mango

Get ready before you start

Jug	Oven	Counter	Ready on stovetop	Plugged in and ready	Preparation required
Boiling with 5 cups of water		Chopping board Sharp chefs knife Serving dishes	Large frying pan Medium pot Medium frying pan	Food processor with grating and slicing attachments	2 cups cooked medium grain brown rice

Timing

:00	CURRY	Cut onions and begin to saute
:03	NOODLES	Put rice noodles on to cook
:05	CURRY	Add spices and other ingredients
:10	COLESLAW	Process vegetables and make dressing
:16	DESSERT	Make coconut rice and slice mango
:23	NOODLES	Drain noodles and add flavours
:25	DESSERT	Plate dessert and garnish
:27	CURRY	Finish with coconut cream and garnish
:29	COLESLAW	Mix with dressing and garnish
:30	FINISH	Serve and enjoy!

Thai Red Curry with Chickpeas

It is so easy to make a Thai curry just by adding some great Thai flavours. Serve over rice noodles.
MAKES 6 X 1 CUP SERVES

Step 1 – Saute Onion

1 onion diced

1 tablespoon oil

2 cloves garlic crushed

2 tablespoons ginger puree

2 tablespoons lemongrass puree

In a large frying pan saute onion, oil, garlic, ginger and lemongrass for around 5 minutes or until soft.

Step 2 – Add Ingredients

2 teaspoons ground coriander

2 teaspoons Thai red curry paste

2 tablespoons water

2 tablespoons liquid honey

1 teaspoon salt

½ green bell pepper (capsicum)

½ red bell pepper (capsicum)

14oz (400g) can crushed tomatoes

2 x 14oz (400g) cans chickpeas (garbanzo beans)

Stir in the ground coriander for around 30 seconds to activate the flavours.

In a cup mix the red curry paste with water and add to the pan.

Add the honey and salt.

Finely slice bell peppers and add to pan.

Add the tomatoes and chickpeas and cook for around 5 minutes until bubbling.

Step 3 – Finish & Garnish

6fl oz (200ml) coconut milk

garnish: cilantro (fresh coriander)

Add the coconut milk and stir in gently for a couple of minutes until heated.

Garnish with chopped cilantro.

Thai Ginger Coleslaw

An amazingly tasty coleslaw!
MAKES 6 X 1 CUP SERVES

3 cups red cabbage thinly sliced

2 cups white cabbage thinly sliced

2 cups carrots grated

2 tablespoons black sesame seeds

½ cup roughly chopped cilantro (fresh coriander)

½ cup Thai Dressing

garnish: cilantro (fresh coriander)

Make the Thai Dressing in the bottom of your serving bowl.

Using a food processor, grate the carrots and slice the cabbage.

Put all the ingredients into the serving bowl and toss with your hands to mix the dressing through.

Garnish with chopped cilantro.

Thai Dressing

This dressing is so full of flavour!
MAKES ½ CUP

2 tablespoons lemongrass puree

1 tablespoon ginger puree

3 tablespoons lemon juice

3 tablespoons lime juice

1 tablespoon liquid honey

½ teaspoon chilli puree

½ teaspoon salt

2 tablespoons sesame oil

Mix with a spoon.

Rice Noodles with Cilantro & Lime Juice

A great way to add some flavour to rice noodles.
MAKES 4 X 1 CUP SERVES

200g (6oz) rice noodles

5 cups boiling water

1 cup chopped cilantro
(fresh coriander)

1 tablespoon oil

½ teaspoon salt

1 tablespoon lime juice

garnish: lime wedges

garnish: cilantro (fresh coriander)

Put noodles in a bowl or pot.

Cover with boiling water and put a plate or lid on top.

Sit for around 5-12 minutes (every noodle is different) or until soft.

Drain in a colander and put noodles back into the bowl or pot.

Mix in remaining ingredients.

Plate and garnish with lime wedges and chopped cilantro.

Sticky Rice Mango

My favourite dessert when in Thailand!
MAKES 4 SERVES

2 cups cooked medium grain brown rice

6fl oz (165ml) coconut milk

2 tablespoons liquid honey

2 tablespoons lime juice

1 large mango

garnish: 1 tablespoon toasted sesame seeds

garnish: 1 lime cut into wedges

Combine the rice and coconut milk in a medium frying pan and simmer for around 5 minutes or until it thickens.

Stir in the honey and lime juice.

Cut two large cheeks from either side of the mango stone. Cut off the skin and cut into smaller slices.

Plate the rice and fan the mango out on top.

Garnish with a sprinkle of the toasted sesame seeds and some lime wedges.

A nice blend of vegetables, quinoa and an amazing goulash for mushroom lovers. The Banana Date Smoothie is something you must try!

**Hungarian
Goulash
with Tofu**

**Lemon Infused
Quinoa**

**Sweet
Chilli Roast
Vegetables**

**Fresh Mexican
Salad**

**Banana Date
Smoothie**

Get ready before you start

Jug	Oven	Counter	Ready on stovetop	Plugged in and ready	Preparation required
Boiling with 3 cups of water	Fan bake 350°F (180°C) 2 oven trays	Chopping board Sharp chefs knife Serving dishes	Large frying pan Medium pot Medium frying pan	Blender	

Timing

:00	ROAST VEGES	Chop and put vegetables in the oven
:06	QUINOA	Put quinoa on to cook – turn down when boiling
:08	GOULASH	Start sauteing chopped onion and mushrooms
:11	SALAD	Make dressing in bowl and add other ingredients
:16	GOULASH	Add most remaining ingredients
:20	QUINOA	Plate up the quinoa
:22	ROAST VEGES	Make dressing, plate vegetables from oven and pour dressing over
:26	SMOOTHIE	Blend the smoothie and garnish
:29	GOULASH	Add coconut cream and garnish
:30	FINISH	Serve and enjoy!

Hungarian Goulash with Tofu

Tofu and mushrooms make a great combination in this dish!
MAKES 6 X 1 CUP SERVES

Step 1 – Saute Onion & Mushroom

1 onion roughly diced

1 tablespoon oil

2 cloves garlic crushed

8oz (240g) mushrooms sliced

In a large frying pan saute onion, oil, garlic, and mushrooms in a pot for 5 minutes until onion is clear.

Lid on is best so mushrooms can sweat.

Step 2 – Add Ingredients

1 tablespoon finely chopped fresh thyme leaves

2 x 14oz (400g) cans crushed tomatoes

1 teaspoon salt

1 pinch cayenne pepper (optional)

1 tablespoon liquid honey

16oz (450g) tofu

Add thyme, tomatoes, salt, cayenne pepper and honey. Stir until heated through and just bubbling.

Cut tofu into ½in (1cm) cubes. Add to the goulash.

Tip: If you don't have fresh thyme simply replace with 1 teaspoon of dried thyme. Dried herbs are generally more potent than fresh so you don't need to use as much. As a guide use 1 teaspoon of dried herbs to 3 teaspoons (or 1 tablespoon) of fresh.

Step 3 – Finish & Garnish

6fl oz (200ml) coconut cream

garnish: cilantro (fresh coriander)

Add coconut cream and tofu and stir in gently.

Taste and adjust cayenne pepper and salt to taste.

Garnish with chopped cilantro.

Sweet Chilli Roast Vegetables

This delicious combination can be served warm as a side dish or chilled as a salad.
MAKES 8 X 1 CUP SERVES

Step 1 – Roast Vegetables

10 cups diced vegetables of your choice:

- pumpkin or butternut
- sweet potato (kumara)
- zucchini (courgette)
- red bell pepper (capsicum)
- red onion

2 tablespoons oil

Dice vegetables into different shapes but keep overall size around 1in (2cm).

Roast vegetables with oil at 350°F (180°C) for about 20 minutes.

When soft (but not mushy) put directly on your serving platter.

Step 2 – Make Dressing & Garnish

2 tablespoons lemon juice

2 tablespoons sweet chilli sauce

1 tablespoon oil

½ teaspoon salt

2 tablespoons whole-grain (seeded) mustard

4 tablespoons water

garnish: Italian parsley

Heat medium frying pan. Add dressing ingredients and stir until bubbling. Add more water if needed to get a ketchup-like texture.

Pour directly over roast vegetables.

Garnish with chopped parsley.

Tip: This salad can be eaten the following day and actually improves with a little time. However I will be very surprised if you end up with leftovers.

Fresh Mexican Salad

The celery seeds really make this salad come alive!
MAKES 8 X 1 CUP SERVES

....

14oz (400g) canned whole kernel sweet corn drained
20 cherry tomatoes halved
1 cup roughly chopped cilantro (fresh coriander)
1 tablespoon celery seeds
4 cups mesclun or spring lettuce mix

DRESSING:
1 tablespoon lime juice
1 tablespoons lemon juice
1 tablespoon olive oil
2 tablespoons sweet chilli sauce
¼ teaspoon salt

In your serving bowl, mix the dressing ingredients.

Add the tomatoes, cilantro and celery seeds and mix.

Sit the lettuce on top.

Gently toss when you are ready to serve.

Banana Date Smoothie

A delicious creamy sweet smoothie.
MAKES 2 X 1 CUP SERVES

....

1 cup almond, soy, oat or rice milk

2 large ripe bananas

10 dried dates

1 cup ice cubes

garnish: nutmeg

Put all ingredients in blender and blend. Make sure you blend the dates well.

Pour into glasses and serve immediately with a garnish of nutmeg.

Tip: You can put dates and some boiling water in the blender and let sit for a couple of minutes until soft before adding other ingredients. This process is not essential but it will be gentler on your blender and will not take as long to blend.

Lemon Infused Quinoa

A quick accompaniment to any hotpot!
MAKES 3 X 1 CUP SERVES

....

1½ cups dry quinoa

3 cups boiling water

½ teaspoon salt

2 teaspoons lemon zest

1 tablespoon olive oil

2 tablespoons lemon juice

2 tablespoons sliced almonds

Put the quinoa in a medium pot with boiling water. Put the lid on and bring back to boil.

Turn the heat down and simmer (just bubbling) for 12 minutes or until the water has disappeared.

Add lemon zest, lemon juice, salt and olive oil and stir in the pot.

Plate and garnish with sliced almonds.

With the salads and fruit kebabs, this is one of the most colourful meals in the series.

Greek Potato Cake

Chunky Avocado & Tomato Salsa

Fresh Pepper Medley

Honey Glazed Carrots

Fruit Kebabs with Cashew & Pear Cream

Get ready before you start

Jug	Oven	Counter	Ready on stovetop	Plugged in and ready	Preparation required
Boiling with 9 cups of water		Chopping board Sharp chefs knife Serving dishes	2 medium pots Medium frying pan	Blender	Purchase kebab sticks (bamboo skewers)

Timing

:00	POTATOES	Put potatoes on to cook
:01	CARROTS	Put carrots on to cook
:02	DESSERT	Prepare fruit and arrange on kebab sticks, cover and put in fridge
:18	MEDLEY	Cut and assemble all ingredients
:21	POTATOES	Prepare mixture and start to fry
:26	CARROTS	Add toppings and plate up
:27	SALSA	Cut and combine all ingredients
:29	DESSERT	Blend all ingredients for Cashew & Pear Cream
:30	FINISH	Serve and enjoy!

Greek Potato Cake

MAKES 8 CAKES

Step 1 – Cook Potatoes

2lb (1kg) white potatoes unpeeled (around 3 large)
6 cups boiling water

Cut potatoes into ½in (1cm) cubes for fast cooking and put in a medium pot with boiling water. Simmer until soft (up to 10 minutes). Drain well.

Step 2 – Make Potato Mash

½ cup thinly sliced sun-dried tomatoes
3 scallions (spring onions) sliced
1 small red onion finely diced
1 teaspoon ground cumin
1 teaspoon salt
½ cup chopped cilantro (fresh coriander)

Mash potatoes roughly so there are still some chunks left.

Thinly slice sun-dried tomatoes and scallions and mix with potato.

Add remaining ingredients to mashed potato and mix well.

Step 3 – Form Cakes & Fry

½ cup sesame seeds
2 tablespoons oil (for frying)
garnish: scallions (spring onions)

Pour the sesame seeds into a shallow bowl.

Measure out ½ cup of the potato mix and roll into a ball with your hands. Press to flatten into a "cake" shape. Roll in the sesame seeds so it is liberally covered. Repeat with remaining potato mixture.

Heat a non stick frying pan with a little oil. Fry cakes for around 3 minutes each side or until lightly brown.

Garnish with sliced scallions.

Tip: Alternatively you can bake these in the oven. Simply brush with a little oil and bake for 20 minutes at 300°F (150°C).

Chunky Avocado & Tomato Salsa

MAKES 2 CUPS

10 cherry tomatoes

1 avocado

½ teaspoon salt

1 tablespoon lemon juice

1 clove garlic

Randomly chop the cherry tomatoes and place in a serving bowl.

Dice the avocado thinly and add to the bowl.

Sprinkle over salt and lemon juice.

Crush garlic and gently combine all ingredients together with your hands.

Fresh Pepper Medley

MAKES 8 X 1 CUP SERVES

3oz (100g) mesclun or spring lettuce mix
½ orange bell pepper (capsicum)
½ red bell pepper (capsicum)
½ yellow bell pepper (capsicum)
4oz (125g) sugar snap or snow peas
1 cup beetroot matchsticks

Place the mesclun in the bottom of your serving bowl.

Finely slice the bell peppers and randomly chop the sugar snap peas.

Add to the bowl and mix gently.

Peel the beetroot and thinly slice. Stack the slices then slice finely to create matchsticks. If the beetroot is juicy, roughly dry with a paper towel. This will help prevent it from staining the other ingredients. Sprinkle the matchsticks over the top of the other vegetables.

Tip: If you prepare the vegetables ahead of time or need to store this salad, make sure it is covered and sprinkle some water through it to keep everything fresh.

Tip: Mesclun is a salad mix of assorted small, young salad leaves. Traditionally specific lettuces were used in equal portions however many other leafy vegetables, such as spinach and arugula are now included.

Fruit Kebabs

MAKES 10 KEBABS

¼ honeydew melon

¼ cantaloupe (orange/rock melon)

¼ small watermelon

½ large mango

20 blueberries

5 large strawberries

½ pineapple

3 kiwifruit

garnish: 2 tablespoons shredded coconut

Turn your chopping board over or use a new board so you do not taint the fruit with savoury flavours.

Use a sharp knife to skin the fruit and chop into 1in (2cm) chunks.

Arrange the fruit on a platter in order of colour (red, orange, yellow, green, blue). Handle the fruit gently to preserve the sharp edges that make it look appealing.

Push the fruit on the skewers. This is a time consuming job so you may want to recruit a helper.

If you are not serving straight away cover with cling wrap and refrigerate.

Sprinkle with shredded coconut just before serving.

Tip: If you refrigerate the fruit overnight it will look fresher for longer at room temperature.

Tip: You will have some leftover fruit pieces that are smaller or out of shape. Just make a fruit salad or smoothie out of these!

Honey Glazed Carrots

MAKES 4 X 1 CUP SERVES

....

16oz (450g) baby carrots pre-peeled
3 cups boiling water
¼ teaspoon salt
2 tablespoons liquid honey
garnish: 1 teaspoon sesame seeds

Put the carrots in a medium pot with boiling water and cook for approximately 10 minutes or until tender.

Drain well and pour into serving bowl.

Add the salt and honey and toss the carrots in the bowl to distribute seasonings evenly.

Garnish with sesame seeds.

Cashew & Pear Cream

This is a lovely all-purpose cream that you can use with many desserts.
MAKES 2 CUPS

14oz (400g) can pears (in juice)
1 cup cashew nuts

Add the pears (with the juice) and cashew nuts to a blender and blend until you have a smooth cream.

Tip: Keep blending until you have a smooth cream – you do not want bits of cashew nuts and juice.

This fresh Mexican combination is similar to what you can find at Mexican restaurants. It is like a burrito without the tortilla! You will love the tangy flavours.

Zesty Lime & Cilantro Rice

Corn & Pepper Fiesta

Guacamole

Fresh Mexican Salsa

Freshly Cut Mangos & Lime Juice

Get ready before you start

Jug	Oven	Counter	Ready on stovetop	Plugged in and ready	Preparation required
Boiling with 3 cups of water		Chopping board Sharp chefs knife Serving dishes	Medium pot Medium frying pan		

Timing

:00	RICE	Put rice on to cook
:01	FIESTA	Make Corn & Pepper Fiesta
:06	GUACAMOLE	Mash avocado and combine all ingredients
:11	SALSA	Cut tomatoes and combine all ingredients
:17	BEANS	Heat beans
:19	LETTUCE	Chop lettuce and place in serving bowl
:21	MANGOS	Cut mango and arrange on dish with lime wedges and mint
:25	RICE	Combine with remaining ingredients and plate up
:29	BEANS	Place beans in serving bowl
:30	FINISH	Serve and enjoy!

Corn & Pepper Fiesta

MAKES 4 X ½ CUP SERVES

2 x 14oz (400g) cans whole kernel sweet corn

1 red bell pepper (capsicum)

3 scallions (spring onions)

1 tablespoon extra virgin olive oil

¼ teaspoon salt

Drain canned corn.

Finely dice bell pepper.

On a diagonal angle finely slice the scallions.

Combine all ingredients in a serving bowl.

Tip: You can use fresh or frozen sweet corn for this recipe. To defrost frozen corn simply run hot water over it for about 30 seconds. You do not need to cook it.

Black Beans

MAKES 4 X ½ CUP SERVES

....

14oz (400g) can black beans
¼ teaspoon salt

Drain beans and heat in a medium frying pan on the stove. Add salt and stir.

Once the beans are heated pour into a separate serving dish.

Freshly Chopped Lettuce

A fresh green accompaniment
MAKES 3 X 1 CUP SERVES

....

3 cups sliced romaine (cos) lettuce

Cut lettuce and put in serving bowl.

Tip: If it looks tired you can rinse it in some cold water to give it some life.

Guacamole

Everyone loves Guacamole. The perfect addition to a Mexican meal.
MAKES 1–2 CUPS

1 large or 2 medium avocados (ripe)

2 tablespoons lemon juice

½ teaspoon salt

¼ red onion finely diced

1 clove garlic crushed

garnish: finely diced red onion

Halve, carefully remove the stones and skin of the avocado and put in a mixing bowl. Mash well with a fork.

Add all other ingredients and stir in. Plate and garnish with red onion.

Tip: I prefer not too much onion in my guacamole, however if you want more texture add more onion. Guacamole can also be made with diced tomato however I have not included it here as tomato is an ingredient in the Fresh Mexican Salsa also served with this meal.

Zesty Lime & Cilantro Rice

MAKES 4 X ½ CUP SERVES

1½ cups long grain brown rice

3 cups boiling water

½ cup finely chopped cilantro (fresh coriander)

zest of one lime finely grated

¼ cup lime juice

½ teaspoon salt

2 teaspoons extra virgin olive oil

In a medium pot combine the rice and boiling water and bring back to the boil.

Put the lid on and turn down the heat and simmer for around 25 minutes or until rice is soft and the water has disappeared. Do not stir.

Remove from the heat.

Combine the remaining ingredients in the pot then spoon onto your serving dish.

Fresh Mexican Salsa

This flavoursome salsa really makes this meal taste great and gives genuine Mexican flavour.
MAKES 2½ CUPS

....

2 cups finely chopped ripe tomatoes

¼ cup very finely diced red onion

½ cup finely chopped cilantro (fresh coriander)

1 red chilli finely diced (optional)

2 small cloves garlic crushed

½ teaspoon salt

4 tablespoons lime juice

garnish: cilantro (fresh coriander)

Chop all ingredients on a chopping board and put in a serving bowl.

Garnish with chopped cilantro.

Freshly Cut Mangos & Lime Juice

It is great to finish a meal with a fresh dessert and the toppings turn mango from good to amazing!
MAKES 4 SERVES

2 mangos
juice of 1 lime
garnish: mint
garnish: 2 limes

For each mango slice longways on one side of the mango stone. Repeat on the other side.

This creates two "cheeks". Cut lines vertically and horizontally to form cubes. Cut so you just get to the skin and be careful not to cut through.

Press out to reveal cubes you can bite off from the skin.

Arrange the four cheeks on the serving dish. Squeeze lime juice on top.

Garnish with lime wedges and finely chopped mint.

This is a great healthy breakfast with hot and cold options!

Swiss Bircher Muesli

Wild Berries

Homemade Almond Butter

Nearly French Toast

Breakfast Potatoes

Get ready before you start

Jug	Oven	Counter	Ready on stovetop	Plugged in and ready	Preparation required
Boiling with 10 cups of water		Chopping board Sharp chefs knife Serving dishes	Medium pot Large frying pan 2 medium frying pans	Blender Food processor	

Timing

:00	POTATOES	Cut both types of potatoes and put on stove top to cook
:03	MUESLI	Combine all ingredients and put in fridge
:06	BUTTER	Pan fry almonds
:07	TOAST	Combine mixture and fry first batch
:13	POTATOES	Fry up potatoes
:17	BUTTER	Process nuts and other ingredients
:20	BERRIES	Prepare fruit, plate up and garnish
:24	TOAST	Finish cooking another batch
:28	POTATOES	Garnish with parsley
:29	MUESLI	Remove from refrigerator, plate and garnish with almonds
:30	FINISH	Serve and enjoy!

Swiss Bircher Muesli

MAKES 3 X 1 CUP SERVES

1 cup quick oats (fine rolled oats)
½ cup raisins
¼ cup sliced almonds (or any chopped nut of your choice)
¾ cup orange juice (2 oranges)
1 cup almond, soy, oat or rice milk
½ cup almond meal
1 medium sized apple
garnish: sliced almonds

Combine all ingredients (except apple) in a mixing bowl.

Grate the apple with a hand grater and mix into the rest of the ingredients.

Put in the refrigerator to cool and thicken.

Plate and garnish with sliced almonds.

Tip: You can use regular rolled oats if you do not have quick oats.

Tip: This recipe is very flexible so do not worry if you are missing an ingredient – except the oats of course! Experiment to come up with your favourite combination remembering that the liquid should be approximately double the quantity of oats. This muesli can be eaten after 5 minutes but it is even better refrigerated overnight.

Wild Berries

MAKES 3-4 CUPS

6 medium-large strawberries
6 oz (170g) blueberries
4 oz (125) raspberries
garnish: mint leaves

Remove green tops then halve the strawberries.

Place all the berries in a serving bowl and gently mix.

Garnish with finely chopped mint leaves then top with sprig of mint.

Homemade Almond Butter

MAKES 2 CUPS

2 cups almonds
2 tablespoons oil
1 teaspoon salt

Pan fry the almonds in 1 tablespoon of oil. Heating the almonds brings out their beautiful flavour and aids the release of their natural oils.

Allow to cool.

Put the almonds, salt and remaining tablespoon of oil into a food processor and blend.

As the nuts are blended the mix will become crumbly in texture. Continue blending and after around 2 minutes the mixture will start to clump up as the nuts release their oils, and will suddenly become almond butter.

Tip: Store in an airtight container in the refrigerator. It will keep for up to a month. You may need to stir before use as the oils will separate due to the lack of chemical stabilisers usually found in nut butters.

Nearly French Toast

MAKES 16 HALF SLICES

¼ cup cashew nuts

1 cup water

½ teaspoon vanilla essence

1 tablespoon liquid honey

¼ teaspoon salt

⅛ teaspoon turmeric

8 slices thick whole grain bread

oil for frying (if needed)

garnish: fresh berries (blueberries, strawberries, boysenberries)

garnish: liquid honey or maple syrup (optional)

Add all ingredients (except the bread, oil and fresh berries) to a blender and blend until smooth.

Make sure you blend the mixture really well so you have a consistent paste rather than water with little cashew nut pieces

Heat a non-stick frying pan. Depending on the quality of your pan, you may be able to get away with using no oil at all. Or you may wish to use a couple of drops to start with.

Cut the bread in half diagonally (you will have 16 pieces total).

Pour the cashew mixture into a bowl and dip each piece of bread in it for a couple of seconds each side to completely coat the bread and soak in.

Place in a medium frying pan and cook for around 2 minutes per side.

Garnish with fresh berries.

Tip: You can also drizzle with honey or maple syrup.

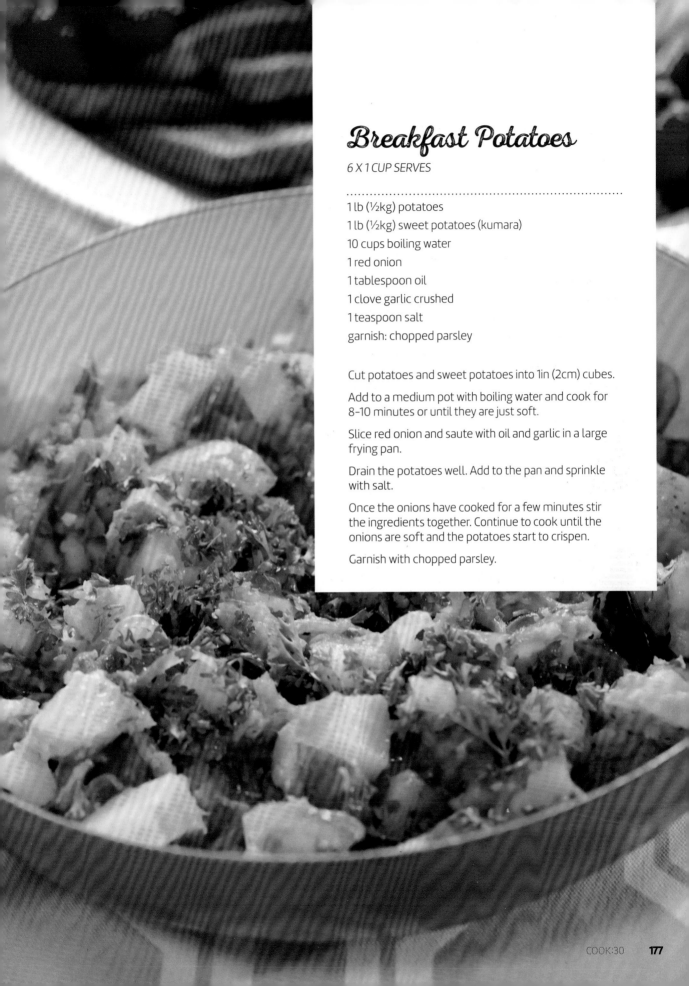

Breakfast Potatoes

6 X 1 CUP SERVES

1 lb (½kg) potatoes
1 lb (½kg) sweet potatoes (kumara)
10 cups boiling water
1 red onion
1 tablespoon oil
1 clove garlic crushed
1 teaspoon salt
garnish: chopped parsley

Cut potatoes and sweet potatoes into 1in (2cm) cubes.

Add to a medium pot with boiling water and cook for 8-10 minutes or until they are just soft.

Slice red onion and saute with oil and garlic in a large frying pan.

Drain the potatoes well. Add to the pan and sprinkle with salt.

Once the onions have cooked for a few minutes stir the ingredients together. Continue to cook until the onions are soft and the potatoes start to crispen.

Garnish with chopped parsley.

This Shepherdess Pie is a great warming winter dish! With some tangy salads and a lovely dessert that is so easy!

Shepherdess Pie

Seedy Slaw

Sesame Cucumber Ribbon Salad

Pineapple Rice Pudding

Get ready before you start

Jug	Oven	Counter	Ready on stovetop	Plugged in and ready	Preparation required
Boiling with 6 cups of water	Fan bake 350°F (180°C) Oven dish	Chopping board Sharp chefs knife Serving dishes	Medium pot Medium frying pan Large frying pan	Blender Food processor with grating and slicing attachments	2 cups cooked long-grain brown rice 2 bananas, peeled, cubed and frozen overnight

Timing

:00	PIE	Chop potatoes and put on to boil
:02	PIE	Saute oil, onion and garlic for Shepherdess Pie filling
:04	SLAW	Make dressing, process vegetables and combine
:11	PIE	Add lentils and tomato sauce to pan
:15	SALAD	Peel cucumber and combine all ingredients
:19	DESSERT	Heat rice and milk
:23	PIE	Mix the potato mash and make the pie
:27	DESSERT	Finish Pineapple Rice Pudding
:30	FINISH	Serve and enjoy!

Shepherdess Pie

SERVES 6-8

Step 1 – Make Potato Mash

2 lb (1 kg) potatoes unpeeled

2 tablespoons sweet chilli sauce

1 tablespoon whole-grain (seeded) mustard

½ teaspoon salt

1 cup almond, soy, oat or rice milk

¼ teaspoon ground turmeric

Chop potatoes into 1in (2cm) cubes. Add to a pot with boiling water and cook for around 10 minutes or until soft. Drain well.

Mash with a potato masher. Leave some chunks of potato for interest rather than getting everything perfectly mashed.

Add remaining ingredients to the pot and stir well.

Step 2 – Make Lentil Mix

½ tablespoon oil

1 large red onion diced

1 large clove garlic crushed

2 cups brown lentils cooked or canned (drained)

2 cups tomato pasta sauce (store bought)

1 teaspoon salt

Saute oil, onion and garlic in a large frying pan for 5 minutes or until the onions are clear.

Add the cooked lentils, tomato sauce and salt. Stir ingredients together and simmer for a few minutes.

Step 3 – Assemble

garnish: parsley

Pour the filling in to an oven dish and spread it out evenly.

Spread mash on top of filling mix.

The pie can be served as it is or baked in the oven at 350°F(180°C) for around 10 minutes to set.

Garnish with finely chopped parsley.

Seedy Slaw

MALES 6 X 1 CUP SERVES

2 cups grated carrot
2 cups finely sliced red cabbage
2 cups finely sliced white cabbage
1 tablespoon white sesame seeds
1 tablespoon black sesame seeds
1 tablespoon celery seeds
1 teaspoon fennel seeds
1 tablespoon poppy seeds
garnish: cilantro (fresh coriander)

Use a food processor with grating and slicing blades to prepare vegetables. You can use a hand grater and knife but it will take longer.

Combine all lemon dressing ingredients in the bottom of the serving bowl and mix with a spoon.

Add slaw ingredients to the bowl and mix with dressing.

Garnish with chopped cilantro.

Tip: Grated beetroot is a great addition to this salad if you want to add some extra colour and an earthy flavour.

Lemon Dressing

MAKES ¼ CUP

¼ cup lemon juice
1 tablespoon liquid honey
1 teaspoon ground cumin
1 tablespoon oil
½ teaspoon salt

Combine all ingredients and mix with a spoon.

Tip: To save dishes, mix the dressing in the serving bowl.

Sesame Cucumber Ribbon Salad

A beautifully delicate and refreshing salad.
MAKES 4 X ½ CUP SERVES

1 medium telegraph cucumber

2 teaspoons sesame oil

¼ teaspoon salt

2 tablespoons lemon juice

1 tablespoon honey

1 teaspoon ginger puree

garnish: 2 baby red bell peppers (capsicum)

garnish: 1 tablespoon sesame seeds

Using a peeler, "peel" the cucumber into long strips/ribbons. When you reach the core (inner part containing the seeds), rotate the cucumber and start "peeling" again. Stop when you have only the small inner part of the cucumber (seed section). Gently transfer the cucumber ribbons to a serving dish.

Combine all the dressing ingredients in a small bowl and mix well.

Pour the dressing over the cucumber.

Garnish with finely sliced (on a diagonal angle) bell peppers and sesame seeds.

Pineapple Rice Pudding

MAKES 4 X 1 CUP SERVES

2 cups cooked long grain brown rice

1 cup almond, soy, oat or rice milk

2 bananas, peeled, cubed and frozen overnight

1 fresh pineapple peeled, cored and roughly diced

garnish: mint

Heat rice and milk in a medium frying pan.

In a blender, blend the banana and ½ the pineapple.

Add the banana/pineapple mix to the pan. Stir well then carefully pour into serving dishes with a small cup.

Chop the remaining pineapple into small pieces. Place on top of rice mix and garnish with mint leaves.

If not serving immediately store in the refrigerator.

Tip: Canned pineapple could be used when fresh pineapple is unavailable or expensive.

Next time you are tempted to visit the local take-out for an unhealthy burger, fries and a thick shake make sure you try this healthy combination instead!

Beefless Burgers

Moroccan Hummus

Sweet Potato Fries

Carob Ice Shake

Get ready before you start

Jug	Oven	Counter	Ready on stovetop	Plugged in and ready	Preparation required
	Fan bake 350°F (180°C) 2 oven trays	Chopping board Sharp chefs knife Serving dishes	Medium frying pan Small frying pan	Blender Food processor	3 bananas, peeled, cubed and frozen overnight

Timing

:00	BURGERS	Cut and put butternut rounds in the oven
:02	FRIES	Cut and put Sweet Potato Fries in the oven
:04	BURGERS	Mix burger ingredients in the food processor and put on to fry
:08	HUMMUS	Saute onions and blend all ingredients
:15	BURGERS	Slice and assemble tomato, lettuce, avocado and buns
:19	FRIES	Remove Sweet Potato Fries from oven, plate and garnish
:24	BURGERS	Assemble burgers and plate up
:27	SHAKE	Put ingredients into blender and blend
:30	FINISH	Serve and enjoy!

Beefless Burgers

These burgers are delicious and you only need to combine ingredients in a food processor to make them!

Step 1 – Roast Butternut

1 butternut pumpkin

1 teaspoon oil

Cut and discard the stalk of the butternut then thinly slice 4 x ¼in (½cm) rounds from the top end (the end without seeds). Leave the skin on.

Put on an oven tray and coat with a little oil.

Bake for 10-15 minutes at 350°F (180°C) or until just soft.

Step 2 – Make Burgers

14oz (400g) can white beans (drained)

10 oz (280g) soy beans or broad beans frozen

½ teaspoon salt

1 teaspoon fennel seeds

1 tablespoon ground coriander

1 tablespoon sweet chilli sauce

3 scallions (spring onions)

1 cup cilantro (fresh coriander) pressed down

1 tablespoon chickpea (besan) flour

Blend all ingredients in a food processor until a solid patty-like mixture is formed. Do not over mix as you do want some texture.

You may need to add a little water or some flour to get the right consistency.

Form the mixture into burger patties using around ½ cup of mixture per burger.

Fry in a medium frying pan with a little oil for around 2 minutes per side or until cooked.

Step 3 – Prepare Additions & Assemble

4 wholemeal burger buns

Moroccan Hummus (next page)

2 large tomatoes sliced

1 avocado sliced

4 leaves of romaine (cos) lettuce

Halve wholemeal buns.

Prepare vegetables.

Assemble the burgers.

Sweet Potato Fries

Wonderfully delicious alternative to French fries.
MAKES 6 X 1 CUP SERVES

3 lb (1½kg) large orange sweet potato (kumara) unpeeled

2 tablespoons oil

1 teaspoon salt

garnish: parsley

Slice the sweet potato into ½in (1cm) round discs. Stack the discs two high then slice into ½in (1cm) fry shapes. Repeat until all the fries are sliced. There is no need to peel the skin off.

In a mixing bowl toss the fries with the oil so they are evenly covered.

Pour the fries onto an oven tray and arrange so they are evenly spaced.

Bake for 20-25 minutes at 350°F (180°C) or until just golden. You want them soft but still holding together. Mix gently every 10 minutes to encourage even cooking.

Sprinkle the salt over the fries, then plate and garnish with chopped parsley.

Moroccan Hummus

MAKES 1½ CUPS

1½ cups finely sliced red onion

1 tablespoon oil

14oz (400g) can chickpeas (garbanzo beans)

4 tablespoons lemon juice

2 tablespoons tahini

1 tablespoon cumin

½ teaspoon salt

½ cup water (possibly more)

2 cloves garlic crushed

In a small frying pan saute the onion and oil for around 5 minutes or until onion is clear. Set aside.

Put remaining ingredients (excluding onion) into a blender and blend until smooth. You may need to add more water.

Pour hummus into serving bowl. Add cooked onion and stir it through.

Carob Ice Shake

Carob is a healthful chocolate alternative as it is naturally sweet and does not contain caffeine.
MAKES 4 X 1 CUP SERVES

3 bananas, peeled, cubed and frozen overnight

4 tablespoons carob powder

2½ cups almond, soy, oat or rice milk

Combine ingredients in a blender and process until smooth. If the blender has difficulty add a little more milk.

Serve immediately.

Tip: These shakes start to melt quickly so you may like to keep in the fridge while you are eating, or make them after you have eaten.

I love soups, and I love trying different soups at the same time. Here are 3 of my favourite soups that you can make individually or all at once for a soup party!

Classic Carrot & Cilantro Soup

Fragrant Thai Tofu Laksa

Creamy Italian Tomato Soup

Fresh Hummus & Wholegrain Bread

Colourful Fruit Platter

Get ready before you start

Jug	Oven	Counter	Ready on stovetop	Plugged in and ready	Preparation required
Boiling with 7½ cups water		Chopping board Sharp chefs knife Serving dishes	2 large frying pans 1 medium pot	Blender Stick blender	

Timing

:00	CARROT	Cut and saute base ingredients
:03	LAKSA	Chop and saute base ingredients
:06	TOMATO	Cut and saute base ingredients
:09	CARROT	Add spices and water and leave to simmer
:11	CREAM	Blend ingredients and reserve
:13	TOMATO	Add remaining ingredients
:15	LAKSA	Add further ingredients
:18	HUMMUS	Combine ingredients in blender and prepare bread
:21	CARROT	Add remaining ingredients and blend
:23	LAKSA	Add tofu and garnish ingredients
:25	SWEET	Assemble fruit platter
:30	FINISH	Serve and enjoy!

Classic Carrot & Cilantro Soup

MAKES 8 X 1 CUP SERVES

Step 1 – Chop & Saute Base Ingredients

1 large onion roughly chopped
2 cloves garlic crushed
5 large carrots roughly chopped
1 tablespoon oil

In a medium pot saute the onion, garlic, carrots and oil until the onions are clear.

Step 2 – Add Spices & Water

½ teaspoon ground nutmeg
1 tablespoon ground coriander
1 tablespoon ground cumin
4 cups boiling water

Add spices and stir for around 30 seconds to activate their flavours.

Add boiling water. Simmer until the carrots are soft.

Step 3 – Make Cashew Cream

1 cup cashew nuts
1 cup cold water

In a blender, blend cashew nuts and water together to make a cashew cream.

Step 4 – Add Remaining Ingredients & Garnish

½ teaspoon salt
2 tablespoons liquid honey
2 carrots grated
garnish: cilantro (fresh coriander)

Add salt, honey and cashew cream to the pot. With a stick blender, blend the soup well.

Bring the soup up to temperature.

Taste and add salt or honey if necessary.

Just before serving grate carrots and stir through the soup for texture.

Garnish with chopped cilantro.

Fragrant Thai Tofu Laksa

MAKES 5 X 1 CUP SERVES

Step 1 – Chop & Saute Base Ingredients

1 cup onion finely sliced

1 tablespoon oil

4 cloves garlic crushed

2 tablespoons lemongrass puree

2 tablespoons ginger puree

In a pot saute onion, oil, garlic, lemongrass and ginger until soft.

Step 2 – Add Ingredients

1 tablespoon ground coriander

½ yellow bell pepper (capsicum)

½ red bell pepper (capsicum)

1 small red onion sliced

1 teaspoon Thai red curry paste

1 tablespoon sesame oil

3 tablespoons liquid honey

8oz (227g) can bamboo shoots

14fl oz (400ml) can coconut milk

1½ cups boiling water

1 teaspoon salt

Add ground coriander to the onion mix and stir through.

Slice the bell peppers very finely and add to the pot.

Add the remaining ingredients.

Stir and increase the temperature to just bubbling (but do not boil as this will cause the coconut milk to separate). Cook for around 7 minutes or until the vegetables are tender and the flavours have combined.

Step 3 – Finish & Garnish

14oz (400g) block firm tofu

2 tablespoons lime juice

garnish: ½ cup roughly chopped cilantro (fresh coriander)

garnish: ¼ cup roughly chopped mint

garnish: lime wedges

Cut tofu in to ½ in (1 cm) cubes. Add to the pot and leave for a couple of minutes to heat and absorb the flavours.

Add lime juice and stir through.

Garnish with cilantro, mint and lime wedges.

Creamy Italian Tomato Soup

MAKES 7 X 1 CUP SERVES

1 large onion chopped

2 tablespoons oil

2 cloves garlic crushed

1 stalk celery roughly chopped

1 small carrot roughly chopped

1 tablespoon dried mixed herbs

3 x 14oz (400g) cans tomatoes

2 cups boiling water

1 tablespoon liquid honey

½ teaspoon salt

1 cup cashew nuts

1 cup cold water

garnish: cashew cream

garnish: Italian parsley sprigs

Saute onion, oil, garlic, celery and carrot in a pot until the onion is clear.

Add all remaining ingredients (except cashew nuts and cold water). Bring to the boil then simmer for 15-20 minutes to let the flavours mingle.

Put the cashew nuts and cold water in a blender and blend to create cashew cream.

Add cashew cream to the pot and stir through (reserve some for garnish).

Blend the soup well with a stick blender in the pot or transfer to a blender if the pot is too shallow.

Garnish with squiggles of cashew cream and sprigs of parsley.

Tip: Almonds may be used as an alternative to cashew nuts in the cream.

Fresh Hummus

MAKES 2 CUPS

....

14oz (400g) can chickpeas (garbanzo beans)

½ teaspoon salt

1 clove garlic crushed

2 tablespoons tahini

4 tablespoons lemon juice

¼ cup water

Put all ingredients in a blender and blend until smooth. You may need to add a little more water to get a pourable consistency.

Taste. Add salt or lemon juice as needed. You should be able to taste every ingredient slightly, with not too much of any single ingredient coming through.

Transfer to a serving bowl and serve with whole grain bread.

Colourful Fruit Platter

SERVES 4-6

....

honeydew melon

cantaloupe (rock melon)

pineapple

watermelon

grapes

Cut the melons and pineapple into quarters (longways) and take out the seeds. Remove core from pineapple. Slice into ½in (1cm) slices. Keep the skin on for ease of eating.

Group together and fan out when putting on the platter. Add grapes at the end.

Tasty Thai curry
on noodles with
a green salad
and cheesecake.
An awesome
combination!

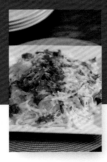

Thai Green Curry Lentils

Zesty Cilantro Rice Noodles

Tuscan Greens Salad

Blueberry Cashew Cheesecake

Get ready before you start

Jug	Oven	Counter	Ready on stovetop	Plugged in and ready	Preparation required
Boiling with 10 cups of water	Fan bake 350°F (180°C)	Chopping board	Medium pot	Blender	
	Oven tray	Sharp chefs knife	Medium frying pan	Food processor	
		Serving dishes	Large frying pan	Stick blender	

Timing

:00	CURRY	Start lentils cooking
:01	CURRY	Cut and put sweet potato in the oven
:03	CHEESECAKE	Process filling, base, make topping, assemble and put in fridge
:13	SALAD	Prepare and combine all ingredients
:18	NOODLES	Put noodles in a bowl with boiling water and cover to cook
:21	CURRY	Add all remaining ingredients including sweet potato and lentils
:28	NOODLES	Drain noodles and add remaining ingredients
:30	FINISH	Serve and enjoy!

Thai Green Curry Lentils

MAKES 6 X 1 CUP SERVES

Step 1 – Lentils & Sweet Potato

1 cup dry brown (crimson) lentils

4 cups boiling water

3 cups sweet potato (kumara) cubed unpeeled

1 tablespoon oil

Add lentils and water to a medium pot, bring to the boil, turn down and simmer for 20 minutes or until the lentils are soft. Drain off any water.

Chop sweet potato into 1in (2cm) cubes. Place on a oven tray and mix with oil.

Bake in the oven at 350°F (180°C) for 15 minutes or until soft.

Step 2 – Add Ingredients

1 onion finely sliced

1 tablespoon oil

2 tablespoons ginger puree

2 tablespoons lemongrass puree

2 cloves garlic crushed

1 red bell pepper (capsicum) diced

1 teaspoon Thai green curry paste

¼ cup water

5 dried kaffir lime leaves

Finely slice the onion into half moons.

In a large frying pan start to saute the onion, oil, ginger, lemongrass and garlic.

Dice the bell pepper into ½in (1cm) cubes and add to the pan.

In a cup mix the green curry paste and water and pour into the pan.

Add the kaffir lime leaves and stir through gently.

Saute for another 5 minutes or until the onion is soft.

Step 3 – Finish

1 teaspoon salt

2 tablespoons honey

6fl oz (165ml) coconut cream

½ cup chopped cilantro (fresh coriander)

Add the salt, honey and coconut cream and stir through.

Add 2 cups of cooked lentils. Freeze or refrigerate any remaining lentils for a future meal.

Add the roasted sweet potato and stir well.

Remove the kaffir lime leaves.

Garnish with cilantro.

Zesty Cilantro Rice Noodles

MAKES 4 X 1 CUP SERVES

8oz (230g) rice noodles

6 cups boiling water

1 cup finely chopped cilantro (fresh coriander)

¼ cup lime juice

zest of 2 limes

¼ teaspoon salt

2 teaspoons oil

garnish: cilantro (fresh coriander)

Put the noodles in a large bowl and cover with boiling water. Cover the bowl with a plate to keep the heat in.

Leave to "cook" for 8-15 minutes or until noodles are just soft.

Drain noodles in a colander and return to the bowl.

Add remaining ingredients and mix together gently.

Plate and garnish with chopped cilantro.

Tuscan Greens Salad

MAKES 6 X 1 CUP SERVES

3oz (100g) baby spinach and arugula (rocket) lettuce mix

2 cups julienne butternut squash or pumpkin (raw)

1 cup cherry tomatoes halved

¼ cup kalamata olives halved

drizzle of olive oil

juice of a lemon

garnish: ¼ cup almonds sliced

Place the lettuce mix into your serving bowl.

Make "rounds" of butternut squash by cutting thin slices (approximately five). Stack the "rounds" and cut off the peel. Slice finely to create julienne strips the size of matchsticks.

Gently combine with the lettuce mix.

Halve the tomatoes and olives and scatter on top of the lettuce mix.

Drizzle with olive oil and lemon juice then sprinkle with sliced almonds.

Blueberry Cashew Cheesecake

MAKES 8 X 1 CUP SERVES

Step 1 – Filling

2 cups cashew nut pieces
1 cup water
½ cup dried dates
¼ teaspoon vanilla essence
pinch of salt

Add the filling ingredients to a food processor and process until you have a very smooth cashew cream. Pour into a bowl and set aside.

Step 2 – Base

1 cup almonds
1 cup cashew nut pieces
1 cup dried dates
½ cup water

Add base ingredients into the food processor (you do not need to wash it) and process until it becomes clumpy in texture. It should have some small pieces of cashew nuts showing. You may need to add a little more water if it is too dry.

With a spoon, press the base firmly into a 10in (25cm) pie dish.

Pour the filling over the base and make it level.

Step 3 – Topping & Finish

3 cups frozen blueberries
2 teaspoons arrowroot
½ cup cold water
1 tablespoon liquid honey (optional)

Pour frozen blueberries into a medium frying pan and heat at a low temperature to defrost.

Mix the arrowroot and cold water in a cup and add to the blueberries.

Stir well until a gel has formed. Add honey if the blueberries need sweetening.

Pour blueberry topping over the cheesecake.

Put the cheesecake in the refrigerator for 15–20 minutes to firm up.

This meal is a tasty blend of different cultures. Includes the dahl (Indian), couscous (Moroccan), and tempeh (Asian).

Tarka Dahl

Lemony Couscous

Tempeh & Cherry Tomato Salad

Pan Fried Asparagus with Sesame Seeds

Peach Ice Smoothie

Get ready before you start

Jug	Oven	Counter	Ready on stovetop	Plugged in and ready	Preparation required
Boiling with 5 cups of water		Chopping board	Large frying pan	Blender	
		Sharp chefs knife	Medium frying pan		
		Serving dishes and glasses	Small frying pan		

Timing

:00	DAHL	Start sauteing onion, garlic, ginger
:03	COUSCOUS	Prepare couscous and set aside to cook
:05	DAHL	Add spices, lentils and water to the pot
:08	SALAD	Cook tempeh, make dressing and assemble other ingredients
:12	ASPARAGUS	Prepare and cook in boiling water
:16	COUSCOUS	Flake with a fork, add remaining ingredients
:19	DAHL	Add remaining ingredients
:22	SMOOTHIE	Blend ingredients and pour into glasses
:26	COUSCOUS	Garnish
:27	DAHL	Garnish with cilantro
:29	ASPARAGUS	Plate up
:30	FINISH	Serve and enjoy!

Tarka Dahl

MAKES 5 X 1 CUP SERVES

Step 1 – Saute Onion

1 onion finely chopped

2 cloves garlic crushed

1 tablespoon oil

4 tablespoons ginger puree

In a large pan saute the onion, garlic, oil and ginger for 5 minutes or until the onions are soft.

Step 2 – Add Spices & Lentils

2 teaspoons ground cumin

2 teaspoons ground coriander

2 teaspoons ground turmeric

1 cup dried red lentils

3½ cups boiling water

Add spices to the onion mix and stir briefly.

Add the lentils and water, stir and simmer for 12–15 minutes or until the lentils are soft.

Step 3 – Finish & Garnish

1 teaspoon salt

2 tablespoons honey

14oz (400g) can chickpeas (garbanzo beans) drained

2 cups frozen green peas

6fl oz (200ml) coconut cream (optional)

garnish: cilantro (fresh coriander)

Stir in remaining ingredients.

Heat through but do not bring to the boil.

Garnish with finely chopped cilantro.

Lemony Couscous

MAKES 6 X 1 CUP SERVES

....

1½ cup couscous (wholemeal)

¼ teaspoon turmeric

½ teaspoon salt

1½ cups boiling water

¼ cup finely chopped parsley

4 tablespoons lemon juice

zest of 1 lemon

2 teaspoons olive oil

Pour couscous into a medium sized mixing bowl.

Add turmeric and salt then stir to distribute evenly.

Pour boiling water over the couscous and stir quickly to avoid clumping.

Immediately cover with a plate. Set aside to cook for 10 minutes. You do not have to cook on the stove as the boiling water will be sufficient.

Check couscous. Ensure all water is absorbed. Fluff gently with a fork.

Add the parsley and lemon juice and stir through.

Plate up and garnish with lemon zest and drizzle with olive oil.

Tempeh & Cherry Tomato Salad

I love the fresh tomatoes and spinach combined with the nutty tempeh and tahini dressing in this salad.
MAKES 4 X 1 CUP SERVES

9oz (250g) pack tempeh

1 tablespoon oil

¼ teaspoon salt

4 cups baby spinach

20 cherry tomatoes halved

TAHINI DRESSING:

4 tablespoons tahini

2 tablespoons lemon juice

¼ teaspoon salt

1 tablespoon liquid honey

4 tablespoons water

Cut the tempeh into ½in (1cm) cubes.

Pan fry the tempeh, oil and salt for around 7 minutes or until golden. Toss or stir often.

Mix tahini dressing ingredients in a small bowl. Stir until smooth. Add a little more water if needed. The dressing should be thick yet pourable.

Place the spinach in a serving bowl and top with tomatoes and tempeh.

Toss salad and drizzle some dressing over the top.

Pan Fried Asparagus with Sesame Seeds

A lovely, quick side dish – a must during asparagus season.
MAKES 2 CUPS

....

14 oz (400g) bunch of asparagus fresh, untrimmed

1 teaspoon oil

¼ teaspoon salt

2 tablespoons sesame seeds

Snap off and discard the woody base from the asparagus spears.

Lightly pan fry the asparagus and oil in a small frying pan.

Sprinkle with salt and sesame seeds.

Peach Ice Smoothie

MAKES 4 X ¾ CUP SERVES

3 bananas
1 cup almond, soy, oat or rice milk
3 cups frozen peaches
¼ teaspoon turmeric
1 tablespoon honey
½ teaspoon vanilla
garnish: slivered almonds

Use a blender to blend all ingredients together.

Pour into glasses and garnish with slivered almonds.

Serve immediately.

Another lovely combination of some popular cafe dishes. Make sure you try the carrot cake balls, you will be pleasantly surprised!

Indian Chickpea & Potato Wraps

Pear & Rocket Salad

Mediterranean Stir Fry Vegetables

Carrot Cake Bliss Balls

Get ready before you start

Jug	Oven	Counter	Ready on stovetop	Plugged in and ready	Preparation required
Boiling with 6 cups of water	Fan bake 350°F (180°C)	Chopping board	Large frying pan	Food processor	
	Oven tray	Sharp chefs knife	Medium pot		
		Serving dishes	Medium frying pan		

Timing

:00	WRAPS	Start potatoes cooking
:02	VEGES	Chop and start to saute vegetables
:06	SALAD	Chop vegetables and combine all ingredients
:12	WRAPS	Make onion mix with potatoes, fold wraps and place in oven
:20	VEGES	Add asparagus and leave on stove to cook
:23	BLISS BALLS	Put ingredients in food processor and roll
:29	WRAPS	Take out of oven, plate up and garnish
:30	FINISH	Serve and enjoy!

Indian Chickpea & Potato Wraps

MAKES 8 WRAPS

Step 1 – Potatoes & Onions

3 large potatoes diced

6 cups boiling water

1 large onion diced

1 tablespoon oil

Cut potato into ½in (1cm) cubes. Put cubes in a medium pot, cover with boiling water and cook for 10 minutes or until soft.

Drain and mash roughly.

In a separate medium frying pan saute the onion and oil until the onion is clear.

Step 2 – Filling

1 teaspoon cumin seeds

1 teaspoon ground turmeric

2 teaspoons ground coriander

2 teaspoons ground cumin

14oz (400g) can chickpeas (garbanzo beans) drained

1 teaspoon salt

1 tablespoon liquid honey

1 cup frozen green peas

Add spices to the onion mix and stir for around 30 seconds.

Drain the potatoes then pour into a large mixing bowl with the chickpeas. Roughly mash.

Add the onion mix and remaining ingredients to the bowl. Mix.

Step 3 – Assemble

8 large tortillas (wraps)

oil for brushing

1 teaspoon white sesame seeds

1 teaspoon black sesame seeds

Place 1 cup of the mixture just below the centre of the tortilla, fold the left and right sides to cover most of the filling. Then fold and tuck in the bottom of the tortilla over while rolling and tucking in the sides.

To summarise: fold, tuck and fold, roll, tuck, roll.

Repeat with the remaining tortillas.

Place wraps on an oven tray. Brush with a little oil and sprinkle over sesame seeds as a garnish.

Bake at 350°F (180°C) for 10 minutes or until crisp.

Pear & Rocket Salad

Arugula (Rocket) has a delicious peppery flavour and makes a lovely salad.
MAKES 6 X 1 CUP SERVES

3oz (100g) arugula (rocket)

2 cups cherry tomatoes (half red, half yellow)

1 pear

1 tablespoon lemon juice

2 tablespoons shredded coconut

2 tablespoons slivered almonds

Place arugula on a serving platter.

Halve the cherry tomatoes and scatter over the arugula.

Quarter the pear and remove the core. Slice into thin strips and place in a small bowl. Mix with lemon juice to prevent the pear flesh browning. Add to the salad and gently and briefly mix ensuring there are plenty of colourful ingredients on top.

Sprinkle over the coconut and almonds as a garnish.

Tip: If the arugula needs livening up splash some water over the leaves before adding the other ingredients.

Mediterranean Stir Fry Vegetables

These summer vegetables really compliment each other well.
MAKES 4 X 1 CUP SERVES

1 red onion thickly diced

1 tablespoon oil

2 cloves garlic crushed

1 red bell pepper (capsicum)

1 yellow bell pepper (capsicum)

1 orange bell pepper (capsicum)

1 zucchini (courgette)

15 stalks asparagus cut into 1in (2cm) pieces

1 teaspoon salt

1 cup halved kalamata olives

garnish: parsley

Saute onion, oil and garlic for a few minutes in a large frying pan on high heat to draw out the sweet flavours.

Cut the bell pepper and zucchini into 1in (2cm) cubes.

Add bell pepper and zucchini to the pan. Continue to saute for around 7 minutes.

Add asparagus and salt. Continue to stir the vegetables until they are soft and cooked but still retaining their shape and colour. Turn heat off.

Scatter the olives over and garnish with chopped parsley.

Carrot Cake Bliss Balls

MAKES 18 MEDIUM BALLS

½ cup dried dates

½ cup raisins

½ cup almonds

½ cup cashew nuts

½ teaspoon clove powder

½ teaspoon cinnamon

½ teaspoon nutmeg

1 cup carrots roughly diced

1 cup quick oats (fine rolled oats)

½ cup almond meal
(ground almonds)

Combine all ingredients (except the almond meal) in a food processor and process until it is a consistent mixture.

You may need to scrape down the sides and re-blend to ensure all the ingredients are well mixed. The mixture is ready if it holds together well when pressed between fingers.

Remove the blade from the food processor. Scoop the mixture out and make balls to the size of your choosing (I like 1½ tablespoon sized balls).

Pour almond meal into a bowl and gently coat the balls in the meal. Allow the carrot colour to be seen by not completely coating the balls.

Tip: You can make your own almond meal by blending almonds in a coffee grinder.

This is a lovely combination of Mediterranean dishes and you will love the healthy Carob "Better Than Ice Cream"!

Dahlatouille

Brown Rice

Chunky Greek Salad

Green Pea & Sesame Mingle

Carob "Better Than Ice Cream"

Get ready before you start

Jug	Oven	Counter	Ready on stovetop	Plugged in and ready	Preparation required
Boiling with 7 cups of water		Chopping board	Large frying pan	Food processor	3 bananas, peeled, cubed and frozen overnight
		Sharp chefs knife	Medium frying pan		
		Serving dishes	2 Medium pots		

Timing

:00	RICE	Put rice on to cook
:02	DAHL	Start cooking lentils
:03	DAHL	Chop vegetables and saute
:09	SALAD	Combine ingredients
:12	MINGLE	Fry vegetables
:14	DESSERT	Put ingredients into food processor and into refrigerator
:19	DAHL	Combine lentils with vegetables
:21	MINGLE	Combine all ingredients and put in serving dish
:24	DAHL	Add remaining ingredients and garnish
:26	RICE	Plate up and garnish
:28	DESSERT	Spoon into serving glasses and garnish
:30	FINISH	Serve and enjoy!

Dahlatouille

This colourful cafe favourite is a cross between a dahl and a ratatouille.
MAKES 8 X 1 CUP SERVES

....

Step 1 – Cook Lentils

1 cup dried red lentils
3 cups boiling water

In a medium pot cook the lentils and water for around 12 minutes or until soft.

....

Step 2 – Add Ingredients

2 tablespoons oil
1 red onion diced
3 cloves garlic crushed
2 tablespoons ginger puree
1 eggplant (aubergine)
2 cups mushrooms
1 zucchini (courgette) diced
1 red bell pepper (capsicum)
1 large stalk celery diced

Put the oil in a large frying pan.

Add the onion, garlic and ginger and start to saute.

Chop the eggplant into ½in (1cm) cubes and add to the pan.

Chop the remaining vegetables into 1in (2cm) cubes and keep adding to the pot one by one.

Saute for around 10 minutes from when you start adding vegetables, or until they are all soft.

....

Step 3 – Finish

1 teaspoons salt
2 tablespoons honey
14oz (400g) can crushed tomatoes
garnish: cilantro (fresh coriander)

Add the cooked lentils, salt, honey and tomatoes to the vegetable mix. Stir and bring to the boil.

Turn down the heat and simmer for a few minutes to let the flavours mingle.

Garnish with chopped cilantro.

....

Brown Rice

Brown rice is much more filling, flavoursome and nutritious than white rice and it's easy once you know how!
MAKES 6 X 1 CUP SERVES

2 cups long grain brown rice

4 cups boiling water

garnish: scallions (spring onions)

Put the rice and boiling water in a medium pot and bring back to the boil.

Put the lid on and turn down the heat and simmer for around 20 minutes or until the water has disappeared.

Spoon into serving dish and garnish with sliced scallions.

Tip: Cook more than you need so you can use for another meal.

Chunky Greek Salad

MAKES 8 X 1 CUP SERVES

3 cups baby spinach

2 cups cherry tomatoes
(half red, half yellow)

½ small red onion

½ orange bell pepper (capsicum)

1 small cucumber

½ cup pitted kalamata olives

1 teaspoon of virgin olive oil

2 tablespoons lemon juice

Place the spinach on a large platter.

Scatter tomatoes and diced onion over the bed of spinach.

Chop bell pepper and cucumber into 1in (2cm) cubes. Gently toss with the other salad ingredients.

Place olives on top of the salad and drizzle over the oil and lemon juice.

Green Pea & Sesame Mingle

MAKES 4 X 1 CUP SERVES

....

2 teaspoons oil
2 cups frozen green peas
2 cloves garlic crushed
3 cups kale finely sliced
½ teaspoon salt
1 tablespoon liquid honey
2 tablespoons toasted sesame seeds

In a medium frying pan saute the peas, garlic, kale with oil and salt for around 5 minutes or until the kale is wilted.

Transfer to a serving bowl and drizzle with honey and sesame seeds.

Tip: You can toast your own sesame seeds in a dry pan or buy them pre-toasted.

Carob "Better Than Ice Cream"

Who would have thought that frozen bananas could become such a delicious, silky, cholesterol-free dessert!
MAKES 4 X 1 CUP SERVES

3 bananas, peeled, cubed and frozen overnight

3 tablespoons carob powder

2 tablespoons liquid honey

1–4 tablespoons cold water (if required)

garnish: ¼ cup frozen raspberries

garnish: mint leaves

Put frozen banana, carob and honey in an s-blade style food processor and blend. It will start off becoming flaky and clumpy. After around 1 minute it will start to combine and all of a sudden it will develop a creamy texture.

If the mixture sticks and avoids the blades, stop the machine and use a spatula to push the lumps down to where the blades will make impact. A couple of tablespoons of water can also assist however too much will make the mixture runny so add with care.

You can store this in the freezer for up to 20 minutes if waiting to serve. However it will turn solid if frozen for any longer.

Serve in dessert glasses and garnish with raspberries and mint leaves.

Tip: If your bananas are really ripe you may not need to add honey. If they are slightly unripe you may need to add more honey.

Tip: This recipe will not work in a liquidiser style blender or with a stick blender.

This is a truly decadent meal that you will love! Basil pesto pasta, fresh salad, flavoursome sweet potato and an amazing dessert!

Mediterranean Sweet Potato

Fresh Garden Salad

Basil Pesto Pasta Salad

Chia Seed Pudding with Black Cherries

Get ready before you start

Jug	Oven	Counter	Ready on stovetop	Plugged in and ready	Preparation required
Boiling with 8 cups of water	Fan bake 400°F (200°C) Oven tray	Chopping board Sharp chefs knife Serving dishes	Medium frying pan Medium pot	Blender Food processor with slicing attachment	

Timing

:00	POTATO	Chop and put sweet potato in oven
:01	PASTA	Put pasta on to cook
:02	PUDDING	Blend ingredients, add seeds and put in refrigerator to set
:05	SALAD	Chop and process ingredients and add dressing
:11	PUDDING	Pour cherries in a bowl and set aside to defrost
:12	PASTA	Drain pasta, make dressing and combine ingredients
:20	POTATO	Make the filling, scoop and refill the sweet potatoes
:26	PUDDING	Put the pudding in glasses with cherries and garnish
:30	FINISH	Serve and enjoy!

Mediterranean Sweet Potato

MAKES 6 SERVES

....

Step 1 – Roast Sweet Potatoes

3 large sweet potato (kumara)

oil for brushing

Cut sweet potato in half and brush the flesh with oil to prevent burning.

Place on an oven tray and bake at 400°F (200°C) for 20 minutes or until soft.

....

Step 2 – Saute Vegetables

1 red onion finely diced

1 tablespoon oil

2 cloves garlic crushed

1 red bell pepper (capsicum) finely diced

1 zucchini (courgette) finely diced

½ teaspoon chilli puree (optional)

¼ cup slivered almonds

½ teaspoon salt

Saute all of the ingredients in a medium frying pan for 5 minutes or until the vegetables begin to soften.

....

Step 3 – Stuff Sweet Potatoes

oil for brushing

garnish: sesame seeds

garnish: cilantro (fresh coriander)

Remove the cooked sweet potatoes from the oven.

Carefully scoop out the centre with a spoon and add the flesh to the pan of vegetables. Mix well.

Fill each of the sweet potato skins with the mixture and heap it up.

Brush lightly with oil and garnish with sesame seeds.

Return to the oven for 5 minutes or until nicely toasted.

Present on a chopping board and garnish with cilantro.

Tip: Leaving a thin layer of flesh inside each sweet potato helps strengthen the skin making it more stable.

....

Fresh Garden Salad

MAKES 6 X 1 CUP SERVES

1 yellow bell pepper (capsicum)

5 baby red bell peppers (capsicum)

7 red radishes

½ cucumber

1 small romaine (cos) lettuce

14 oz (400g) can black-eyed peas

¼ cup chopped cilantro (fresh coriander)

¼ cup chopped mint

a drizzle of olive oil

2 tablespoons lime juice

Cut the ends off the vegetables and remove the seeds from the bell peppers.

Set up your food processor with the thinnest slice blade you have. Put the bell peppers, radishes and cucumber through the processor.

Using a knife remove the end of the lettuce and cut the leaves into 1in (2cm) slices and lay on a serving platter.

Spread the vegetables from the food processor over the lettuce.

Drain can of peas. Add peas and chopped herbs. Gently toss the salad.

Drizzle with oil and lime juice.

Basil Pesto Pasta Salad

MAKES 4 X 1 CUP SERVES

2 cups wholemeal spiral pasta

8 cups boiling water

1 cup cherry tomatoes

1 large avocado

PESTO DRESSING:

1 cup basil pressed down

1 cup cilantro (fresh coriander) pressed down

¼ cup extra virgin oil

½ teaspoon salt

¼ cup lemon juice

½ cup cashew nuts

Bring water to boil in a medium pot, add pasta and cook for around 8 minutes or until pasta is al dente (firm but not hard). Or cook to packet instructions. Drain well.

Combine dressing ingredients in a blender. Blend until smooth.

Pour over pasta and gently stir through.

Halve the tomatoes, add to the pasta and stir briefly.

Transfer salad to the serving bowl.

Dice avocado and scatter on top.

Tip: You can use any wholemeal pasta shape for this recipe like shells, fusilli, macaroni or fettuccine.

Chia Seed Pudding with Black Cherries

This decadent dessert tastes as good as it looks – and it is so healthy with the chia seeds!
MAKES 4 X ¾ CUP SERVES

Step 1 – Mix Ingredients

3 cups frozen black cherries
(pitted)

½ cup dried dates

½ cup cashew nuts

5 tablespoons carob powder

2½ cups water

½ cup chia seeds

Place the cherries in a bowl and set aside to defrost.

Add dates, cashew nuts, carob powder and water to a blender and blend well. Pour into a bowl.

Add the chia seeds to the mixture and stir through reasonably quickly to avoid the seeds clumping together.

Put in the refrigerator for up to 20 minutes so the chia seeds can swell and the mixture will thicken.

Step 2 – Present & Garnish

garnish: sliced almonds.

Place ½ cup of cherries into each glass (or serving dish). Carefully spoon in 1 cup of the pudding and top with more cherries.

Garnish with sliced almonds.

Tip: Chia seeds can differ in "swellability" so you may need to add more to achieve the right consistency.

Tip: This dessert presents well in glassware. I have used large stemmed glasses here.

Tip: If you cannot find frozen cherries you can use frozen blueberries or raspberries.

Falafel is a Middle Eastern food and is a great ingredient to add to wraps. Plus you will love this healthy take on potato wedges and a decadent Banoffee Pie.

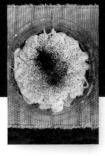

Turkish Falafel Wraps

Tahini Dressing

Spanish Smoked Potato Wedges

Healthy Banoffee Pie

Get ready before you start

Jug	Oven	Counter	Ready on stovetop	Plugged in and ready	Preparation required
Boiling with 4 cups of water	Fan bake 400°F (200°C) Oven tray	Chopping board Sharp chefs knife Serving dishes	Medium frying pan	Food processor	Pre-soak overnight 1 cup chickpeas (garbanzo beans)

Timing

:00	WEDGES	Cut potatoes into wedges, season and put in oven
:03	PIE	Make topping, filling, base; assemble and put in refrigerator
:13	WRAP	Make falafel mix and start to fry, turning as needed
:19	WRAP	Slice salad vegetables and arrange with wraps on platter
:24	DRESSING	Mix dressing ingredients and plate up hummus
:28	WEDGES	Plate and garnish wedges
:30	FINISH	Serve and enjoy!

Turkish Falafel Wraps

Served with salad vegetables, store bought hummus and a tahini dressing
MAKES 24 FALAFEL PATTIES

Step 1 – Blend Mixture

1 cup soaked chickpeas (garbanzo beans) drained

2 cups shelled edamame (green soybeans)

1 teaspoon salt

1 cup roughly chopped cilantro (fresh coriander)

4 tablespoons chickpea (besan) flour

2 large cloves garlic crushed

1 onion chopped into chunks

2 teaspoons cumin powder

Add all ingredients into a food processor.

Process until you have a consistent mix.

Tip: This recipe uses soaked (but not cooked) chickpeas. These must be soaked overnight. You can use a can of cooked chickpeas however this will result in a softer mix and less authentic falafel.

Step 2 – Form & Fry Falafel

1 tablespoon oil

1 package of store bought hummus (or make your own)

Tahini Dressing (see next page)

4 whole wheat tortillas

Remove the blade. Spoon out a ball of mixture about the size of 2 tablespoons. Form into balls with your hand and flatten.

Shallow fry in a non-stick frying pan with the oil for around 2 minutes per side or until golden.

Serve the falafel with salad vegetables, Tahini Dressing and store bought hummus in whole wheat tortillas/wraps. Wrap up and enjoy!

Tip: The falafel harden after they are cooked so are best eaten straight away. You could make the mixture (even a double batch) in advance and immediately refrigerate then fry the falafel just before your meal.

Tip: You may like to warm the tortillas in the oven for a couple of minutes, but do not dry them out.

Tahini Dressing

A lovely dressing that you can use in place of mayonnaise and aioli.
MAKES 1 CUP

....

4 tablespoons tahini

4 tablespoons lemon juice

½ teaspoon salt

1 tablespoon honey

up to 4 tablespoons water

Add all ingredients to a small serving bowl and stir until smooth.

Add water as necessary to get a smooth pourable texture.

Spanish Smoked Potato Wedges

MAKES 4 X 1 CUP SERVES

7 small potatoes

1 tablespoon oil

¾ teaspoon salt

2 teaspoons smoked paprika

garnish: parsley

Cut each potato in half longways and then cut into wedges by cutting through the round part back to the centre of the potato.

In a bowl mix the potatoes with the oil, salt and smoked paprika.

Put on an oven tray, spread out and bake at 400°F (200°C) for around 25 minutes or until golden brown.

Plate in a serving bowl and garnish with parsley.

Healthy Banoffee Pie

MAKES 10 SERVES

Step 1 – Make Cashew Cream

1 cup cashew nuts
½ cup water

Put the topping ingredients in a food processor and process until you have a smooth cream. Pour into a container and set aside.

Step 2 – Base

1 cup cashew nuts
1 cup almonds
1 cup dates dried
½ cup water

Add the base ingredients to the food processor (no cleaning required) and process until it starts to clump together.

Spoon into a round 10in (25cm) pie dish and press down over the base of the dish and around the sides.

Step 3 – Filling & Assemble

2 cups dates dried
¼ tablespoon peanut butter
½ cup water
2 bananas
garnish: 1 tablespoon
carob powder

Combine the dates, peanut butter and water in the food processor (no cleaning required) and process until smooth.

Carefully spoon over the base.

Peel the bananas and slice them on a diagonal angle. Lay the slices on top of the filling.

Spoon the cashew cream over the banana slices.

Place the pie in the refrigerator for 15 minutes to allow it to firm up.

Garnish with a sprinkle of carob powder just before serving.

Tip: In the unlikely event you have leftovers, store in the fridge to keep everything firm as it will soften at room temperature.

This meal is a fresh combination of some Mexican dishes and a lovely Chick Bread and Wild Berries for dessert!

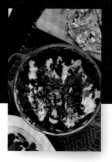

Chilli Con Haba Hotpot

Cilantro Brown Rice

Mexican Tomato, Corn & Avocado Salad

Broccoli Chick Bread

Wild Berries with Cashew Pear Cream

Get ready before you start

Jug	Oven	Counter	Ready on stovetop	Plugged in and ready	Preparation required
Boiling with 4 cups of water		Chopping board	Large frying pan	Blender	
		Sharp chefs knife	Medium pot		
		Serving dishes	Medium frying pan		

Timing

:00	RICE	Put rice and boiling water in a pot and cover
:02	HOTPOT	Cut and saute onions and other ingredients
:05	CHICK BREAD	Make mixture and start cooking
:10	SALAD	Chop and combine all ingredients
:15	HOTPOT	Add remaining ingredients
:19	WILD BERRIES	Blend cream and top with berries
:24	RICE	Mix in remaining ingredients and plate up
:27	HOTPOT	Add garnish
:28	CHICK BREAD	Plate up on board
:30	FINISH	Serve and enjoy!

Chilli Con Haba Hotpot

MAKES 5 X 1 CUP SERVES

Step 1 – Saute

1 onion diced

1 tablespoon oil

2 red bell peppers (capsicum) finely diced

1 red chilli, deseeded and very finely diced (optional)

2 cloves garlic crushed

In a large frying pan saute all the ingredients for around 5 minutes or until the onion is soft.

Step 2 – Add Ingredients

2 teaspoons smoked paprika

14oz (400g) can crushed tomatoes

4 tablespoons tomato paste

14oz (400g) can red kidney beans (drained)

2 tablespoons liquid honey

1 teaspoon salt

Stir in the smoked paprika for around 30 seconds.

Add the remaining ingredients and stir. Heat until just bubbling.

Step 3 – Garnish

¾ cup cashew nuts

1 cup water

garnish: cilantro (fresh coriander)

garnish: 2 baby red bell peppers (capsicum) sliced

Put cashew nuts and water in a blender and blend until smooth to make cashew cream.

Drizzle the cashew cream on top. Garnish with chopped cilantro and sliced bell peppers (or finely sliced red chilli, if you are brave).

Tip: Before garnishing the hotpot you may want to stir in a little water to adjust the texture if it is too thick.

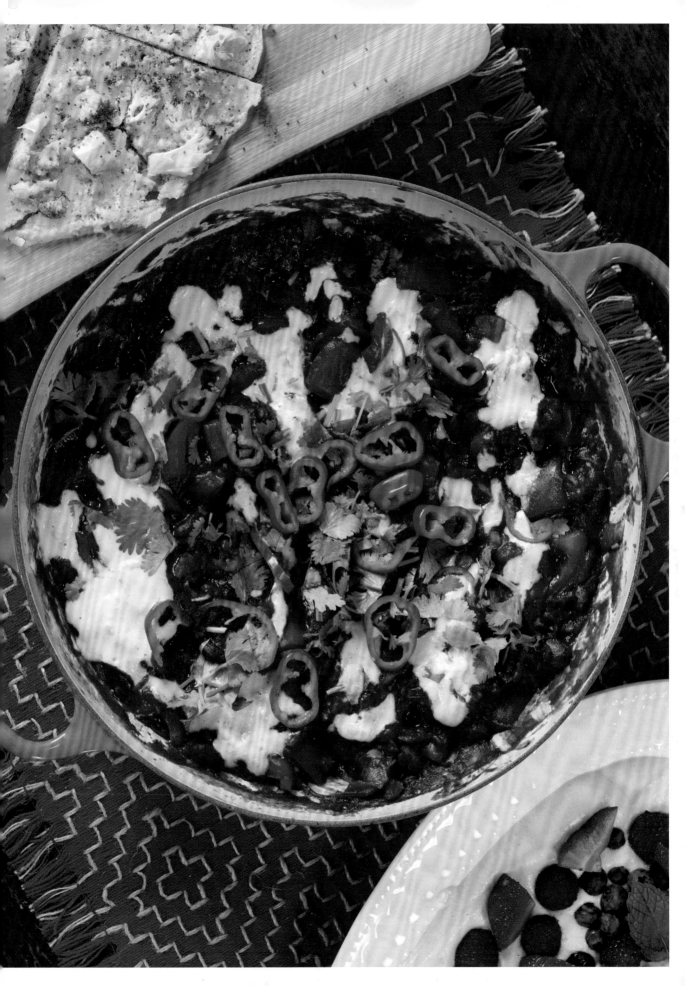

Cilantro Brown Rice

Cooked brown rice can be served as is, especially if it is accompanying a tasty hotpot, however it can be nice to add a few simple ingredients to make it a little bit special.
MAKES 4 X 1 CUP SERVES

2 cups long grain brown rice

4 cups boiling water

¼ teaspoon salt

a drizzle of olive oil

1 tablespoon lemon juice

garnish: cilantro (fresh coriander)

Add the rice and boiling water to a medium pot and put the lid on.

Bring back to the boil, turn down and simmer for 20 minutes or until the water has disappeared.

Transfer the rice to a serving bowl. (Reserve spare rice for another meal). Sprinkle salt over and drizzle with olive oil.

Drizzle lemon juice over the rice. Garnish with chopped cilantro.

Mexican Tomato, Corn & Avocado Salad

MAKES 4 X 1 CUP SERVES

1 cup red cherry tomatoes

14oz (400g) can whole kernel sweet corn (drained)

½ small red onion

1 avocado

2 tablespoons lime juice

2 teaspoons extra virgin olive oil

garnish: cilantro (fresh coriander)

Slice the cherry tomatoes in half and add to a serving bowl.

Add sweet corn and finely diced red onion.

Halve and remove stone and skin from avocado, dice into ½in (1cm) cubes and gently place over the top of the salad.

Drizzle lime juice and oil over the salad, especially the avocado, as this helps prevent it from going brown.

Gently mix ingredients together with your hands.

Garnish with chopped cilantro.

Broccoli Chick Bread

MAKES 4 SERVINGS

½ cup chickpea (besan) flour
½ cup water
½ teaspoon salt
¾ cup finely chopped raw broccoli
1 teaspoon oil
1 teaspoon poppy seeds

In a mixing bowl, mix the flour and half the water until smooth. Then add salt and the rest of the water and mix until combined.

Add the chopped broccoli and stir through.

Heat a medium non-stick frying pan and add oil.

Pour mixture into the pan and swirl around so the base of the pan is evenly coated. Turn the heat down to low and leave to cook for around 5 minutes or until the base of the bread is golden and crispy and the top has set.

Once the bread has cooked, carefully slide from the pan on to a small wooden board for serving.

Sprinkle with poppy seeds and cut into wedges.

Wild Berries with Cashew Pear Cream

MAKES 4 X 1 CUP SERVES

14oz (400g) can pears (in juice)
1 cup cashew nuts
1 cup blueberries
1 cup raspberries
5 large strawberries quartered
garnish: mint

Pour the can contents (pears and juice) and cashew nuts into a blender. Blend until smooth to create the cream.

Pour cream over the base of a serving platter.

Sprinkle the berries evenly on top of the cashew cream.

Garnish with mint leaves.

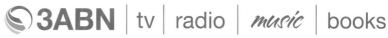

IF YOU LIKE THE COOK:30 RECIPES, YOU WILL LOVE THE REVIVE CAFE COOKBOOKS!

These cookbooks by Jeremy Dixon inspired the Cook:30 series!

Over 70 delicious recipes per book.

Each with 192 pages, full colour photographs.

Most of the recipes in this Cook:30 book are in the Revive Cafe Cookbooks, however they do contain over 200 different recipes not in the Cook:30 book.

Each book also has step-by-step guides so you can customise and piece together your own unique recipes.

View recipe contents and sample pages at www.revive.co.nz.

Available from:
All good booksellers
www.revive.co.nz
www.amazon.com

The books contain wholefood, plant-based receipes.
Except for book 1 and 2 which have a handful of recipes that use eggs and /or feta cheese.

Index